CW00530164

HOW CA. .-DUALITY
HELP ME NOW?

by the same author
Awakening to Self-Knowledge
Living Beyond Fear
The Illumined Understanding
Realising the Truth at the Centre of Life

HOW CAN NON-DUALITY
HELP ME NOW?

Berta Dandler

Shanti Sadan
London

First published 2022

Copyright © Shanti Sadan 2022
29 Chepstow Villas
London W11 3DR

shantisadan.org

All rights reserved.

No part of this publication may be translated, reproduced or
transmitted in any form or by any means without the written
permission of the publisher.

ISBN 978-0-85424-078-4

Contents

Preface

Non-duality in theory and practice offers a fresh and unique approach to the questions that present themselves to thoughtful people in search of fulfilment and inner security.

Scientific investigation has brought an understanding of the natural world which depends on a division between the observer and the observed. Philosophy tries to understand truth, reality and goodness, working within the constraints of the operations of the intellect. Religion proposes a relationship between humanity and the supreme Being based on love and faith.

Non-duality recognises what is valid in all three approaches, and draws upon their insights and vocabularies. Like science, non-duality involves careful investigation guided by well-established principles; like philosophy, it applies reason in drawing inferences from our experience. And like religion, non-duality offers due reverence to that which lies beyond the power and scope of the unillumined human mind.

The aim of the non-dual enquiry is to overcome the divisions between the world as it appears through the workings of our mind and the reality independent of the mind. This is possible because of certain essential truths: the parts inhere within a whole and reality is untouched by individualised perspectives. We find no discontinuity between our own existence and the existence in all, and our consciousness has none of the delimiting features that belong to the objects it is conscious of. Here opportunities arise for an exploration of universality.

Central to non-duality in practice is to calm and refine the mind so that it reflects and does not obscure the reality behind it. In this process, all the mental, emotional, aesthetic and active aspects of the human personality are engaged. As well as opening up the path of transcendental discovery, the practices help us to meet the challenges of life and appreciate the legitimate pleasures offered by the world.

Many of the chapters in this book began as presentations given by the Warden of Shanti Sadan in response to enquiries and requests for guidance and clarification. In some cases the opportunity has been taken to enlarge them for this publication.

What is Non-duality?

The question 'What is non-duality?' is really about 'What am I, in my true nature, and how do I fit into this vast world and find real happiness and fulfilment?' It leads directly into the path of non-dual enquiry and practice.

Perhaps we have heard that non-duality is a kind of philosophy, and that this philosophy is connected to practices like meditation, which together can lead to the possibility of what is called enlightenment. There is truth in this, although we have to add that this comment can only be a pointer. The fact that it is expressed in words means that it cannot be the complete truth, which is beyond the range of words.

Non-duality is rewarding as an approach to subjects like philosophy and psychology. And if we are drawn to a practical path of self-realisation, then understanding the essential non-dual teachings will be a real step on the way to the goal of inner illumination.

We can think about non-duality in three ways:

as a philosophical principle
as an experience
as a practical guide in daily life.

Let us consider our three ways, first in a brief overview, and then in more detail.

As a philosophical idea, non-duality means that the highest truth is that there is one reality, without limit, without qualities, without any divisions within itself, or between itself and anything other than itself, because there is nothing other. It is one without a second, non-dual. Speaking relatively, we can think of the non-dual reality as that which is real and lasting underlying the changing appearances that we experience, and which is the ultimate source of those appearances.

Considering non-duality as an experience, we can say that it is the experience of complete inner independence and wholeness, of being identified with the source of everything. What kind of experience can this be? It is an experience of such fullness that, as an Upanishad says: 'one sees nothing else, one hears nothing else, one thinks nothing else, and understands nothing else'. It is the ultimate satisfaction which leaves behind no quest or question.

Thirdly, we can consider non-duality as a guide on how to live well. Does non-duality have practical relevance? Does it make a difference to life? Can it help us to gain useful knowledge and find lasting fulfilment? The answer to these questions is definitely yes.

One ethical and practical application of non-duality concerns the subject of fear, and this is illustrated by a mythological story from an Upanishad.

The story goes back to the beginning of time, before the world was peopled, apart from one man who was its only inhabitant. Suddenly the man was overpowered by the sense of being alone; he was smitten with fear.

Then he came to himself, and thought: 'If there is none other than me, why should I be afraid?' Fear is always based on the belief that there are others who may pose a threat. But where there is no other, there are no grounds for fear. Realising this, all fear was dispelled.

As the story suggests, we are subject to fear as long as we believe that there is anything over and above our self that could do us harm. In the non-dual experience of reality, which reveals the nature of our true Self, there is no other, so there is no possibility of fear.

Now let us take a more detailed look at our three approaches to non-duality.

When we think of non-duality as a philosophical idea, what we mean is that non-duality is knowledge. And it is a special kind of knowledge which differs from other kinds of knowledge in essential ways.

Our usual way of knowing is through our senses, which are in contact with our body and the world around us, and our mind, which synthesises what we experience. As we know, our senses are sensitive to only a fraction of everything that exists. And our brain and mind are limited in the amount of information they can manage, so they present us with selected aspects of reality.

This is how duality arises. Our mind creates a difference, a two-ness, between itself and everything it experiences, between subject and object.

And from this duality arises multiplicity: out of the reality that is undivided and formless, we experience space and time and countless forms and qualities. And thus we seem to live amongst a multitude of others, and of occasions for fear. Because of these divisions, ordinary knowledge, which includes our life experience and scientific discoveries, can never be complete or final.

We might conclude that true knowledge of reality is impossible. Many philosophers and scientists have inclined to this view. But non-duality holds out a further possibility, that of uncovering in ourselves a different kind of knowledge. In this higher knowledge there are no dualities or gaps, because it does not come through the mind's usual ways of working.

How can there be knowledge which does not involve the workings of the mind, and where there is no division between what is known and the knower?

It is possible because one of the great truths expressed in the non-dual philosophy is that the nature of ultimate reality is pure consciousness.

This consciousness is universal, and our own consciousness is an apparent fragment of that universal consciousness, but in truth identical with it. This identity may be realised when consciousness is distinguished from everything we are conscious of.

This consciousness is the ultimate light in which all our experiences occur. It is our own true Self and the highest Self-knowledge is to know our Self as that consciousness. The possibility of this direct knowledge is a hidden potentiality within us.

This potentiality can be awakened, and this leads to our discussion of non-duality as experience.

What we need to do is to learn to distinguish between awareness itself and the objects of which we are aware. If we can realise that our true Self is not the mind but that fundamental consciousness, then we shall attain to that special kind of knowledge where there are no divisions or separations. There is only the immediacy of experience itself. It is therefore through contemplating our own consciousness, which is also our own being, that we can approach the supreme reality.

How do we awaken the potential for higher knowledge and approach this direct experience? The path begins with hearing the non-dual teachings, and recognising their significance. Then the task is to create conditions in our inner world which help us to become aware of the essential distinction between consciousness and the objects we are conscious of, between our true being and the passing experiences.

This is why the teachers of non-duality and all the genuine wisdom traditions put such a high value on the ability to create inner stillness. The non-dual practices, including meditation, empower us to moderate the restless and often random thinking processes, and create deep inward peace. It is in this peaceful inwardness that higher knowledge awakens and reveals the fundamental reality, the one without a second.

Finally let us consider how non-duality can serve as a guide in life.

Non-duality is the foundation of ethical principles that foster the well-being of the individual and the community. The more we distinguish between our consciousness and what we are conscious of, and think of our self as that consciousness, the more we will recognise the same consciousness as the self of those around us. We will realise that the apparent differences between us belong to the level of appearances, not to what we are in our true nature.

In the light of these teachings we will see that our own highest well-being and happiness come from living in a way that affirms our identity with the conscious reality in all. Then it is clear that to harm another is to harm oneself.

In this way, the great metaphysical principle of non-duality is also a firm and practical basis for ethical living. It shows why and how we should love truth above all. It enables us to live efficiently in the world because we shall see things in their right perspective. If we train our mind in peace and discernment, and turn our sense of what we are from the passing experiences to the inner light, we will discover that the source of all power and strength is the underlying Reality, our own innermost Self. This is why the realisation of non-duality is the supreme relief and fulfilment.

If Non-duality is True, Why is Meditation Needed?

The value of meditation is widely recognised. In various forms it is used in all the world's wisdom traditions. Still, if we have tried meditation, or heard about the principles it is based on, we may have found ourselves asking why regular meditation is necessary or even desirable.

Evidently, meditation takes practice and effort. But the aim is said to be a happy state of effortlessness. And meditation means restraining the movements of the mind, while the goal is complete inner freedom. We might wonder how the means can be so different to the end.

In the case of meditation based on non-duality, another question arises. Non-duality teaches that our true nature transcends the limitations of the mind, and is at one with the essential reality in all, and free of imperfections. The meditations affirm that this is the

9

truth of our deeper nature right now. As we reflect on this, we may ask: If the self is free and infinite even now, why is it necessary to do meditation, or any other practices? Are we not contradicting the view that our true nature is ever perfect by saying that there is something we have to do? Are we not making a gap between our true self and what we feel ourselves to be now, where we have just said there is no gap? Let us consider these questions.

Regarding the need for effort, we might remind ourselves that in life we have been led through many efforts on the way to effortlessness. At one stage, most babies can move around effectively crawling on all fours. But something compels them to struggle up onto their two unsteady legs! This costs many bumps and delays, but eventually most learn to walk with effortless ease.

Learning to speak, to write, to type, to drive, we have passed through similar experiences. If we have learned an art, or sport, or craft, we know how much effort is required to achieve effortlessness. And so it is by voluntarily restraining ourselves that we gain new freedom. The ability to think clearly, to listen deeply, to love unselfishly, are life-enhancing arts, and to develop them we must withhold our immediate reactions, while our sensitivity and awareness heightens.

All these cases involve a contraction followed by expansion. And so it is no surprise that the same principle applies in meditation. By temporarily focusing our attention one-pointedly on an idea that indicates our true nature in meditation, we can find a way through the net of thoughts and moods to the boundless reality and the fulfilment of Self-discovery.

Let us turn to the question of whether it is a contradiction to say that something has to be done in order to realise what is already true. The ultimate Truth is that our innermost Self is not other than the reality underlying the universe. If this is not our experience, then somehow we have lost touch with our real nature and become convinced that our self is the body and mind. This 'not-being-awake-to-our-true-nature' is the root cause of our inability to find lasting happiness in life.

But there is a solution. It is a right understanding of what is most essential to us: our consciousness.

It is to know the distinction between consciousness, which is our self, and everything we are conscious of, which is not-self. The mind, with all its contents, is experienced, so it is not our self. In truth, consciousness and the mind are as different as light and darkness. Consciousness is self-luminous; it needs no other light to reveal it. The mind, by contrast, has no light of its own; without the light of consciousness to reveal the mind, there would be no experience. And consciousness, like light, is one and the same in all beings. This is the ultimate Self of all. Separations and limitations appear in the mind, in the not-Self.

Why do we usually fail to distinguish between self and not-self if the difference is so clear? It is because of the fact that consciousness reveals experience, but never appears as something in experience. So consciousness lights up our mind, but instead of knowing 'I am the conscious Self', our experience is 'I am the mind'. This is why meditation is needed.

To understand in theory that the true Self is beyond the mind and perfect is not enough, so long as we still feel 'the mind is all that I experience—the mind is what I am.'

To withdraw the sense of 'I am' from the mind, and to identify with the light of Self, requires active, sustained application. This is meditation.

There might be something in us which would like to believe that the goal of illumination is attainable without further effort. But this is the mind speaking, not wisdom.

The seeming fusion of consciousness and phenomena is at the heart of the human condition. To know the true nature of consciousness as the universal self-luminous Reality and Self of all is life's greatest and most rewarding purpose.

The path begins with learning to calm and focus the mind. This is the key to relaxation, concentration and resourcefulness. By these means we learn how to distinguish the activities of the mind from the light of awareness that illumines them. This opens the way to an expansion of consciousness and well-being beyond the range of words and thoughts.

Let us now turn from theory to practice. What follows is an example of a set of practices based on the non-dual teachings, which can be taken up and used on a daily basis.

Inner Preparation

The purpose of this preparation is to make an adjustment. Usually, the mind has to be active. As we live our lives and deal with the world, the mind is busy working things out and making things happen. In meditation, the role of the mind is different. It is no longer entirely in charge and outward-facing. The mind's first task now is to be still and transparent, with the attention turned within. There are many ways of making this adjustment. Here is one: for a minute or two, repeat these words inwardly to yourself and focus on their meaning.

> O my mind, you are like a wave in the sea of Reality. Be calm, be still. This is the way to knowledge and well-being.

Breathing Practice

This practice is in two phases, each to be done for two to three minutes.

1. Breathe a little more slowly and deeply than usual.
    If possible, breathe through the nose. Be aware of
    your breathing and try to make the in- and out-
    breaths the same length. As you breathe in, feel
    that the breath is being drawn up, as it were, from
    the region of the navel to the point between the
    eyebrows. Hear the sound of the breath entering
    the body. Then breathe out consciously, bringing
    the attention back to the region of the navel,
    hearing the sound of the breath passing out of
    the body.

2. Keeping up the rhythm of the breathing, after
    each in-breath pause for a moment with the atten-
    tion on the forehead, and after each out-breath,
    again pause for a moment, with the attention at
    the region of the navel, before breathing in again.

Visualisation

The practice is in three stages, each lasting for two
minutes.

1. Visualise yourself from the outside, as it were. Try to see yourself sitting as you are now. Just look at yourself, as you might look at any other person. You are an onlooker, seeing this person in front of you. Practise keeping your attention focused. If distracting thoughts appear, as soon as you notice, come back to the image of yourself.

2. Visualise yourself with a bright light shining from your forehead in all directions. Again, if the attention wanders, bring it back, gently and firmly to the sight of yourself and the bright light shining from the forehead in all directions.

3. See the light spreading in all directions becoming brighter and brighter, so that everything else disappears in that light. All that is left is light.

Meditation on a Text

> AS A WAVE IS AT ONE WITH THE
> SEA, SO IN MY TRUE NATURE I AM
> ONE WITH THE INNERMOST SELF
> OF ALL.

Repeat the text a few times to yourself until the meaning is in focus, then keep your attention on that. Repeat the text, or part of it, whenever you need to bring it back into focus. Do this for five minutes, or the time you have chosen for yourself.

Closing Practice

We began our meditation with an inner preparation, and it is good to close with another adjustment. Consciously beginning and ending the practices helps to make meditation part of the daily rhythm of our lives. We will resume our roles and responsibilities in the world, but now there will be an undercurrent of awareness of the deeper truth on which we have been meditating.

Close the meditation by spending a few moments offering thoughts of unconditional goodwill to all, without exception, based on an awareness of the oneness that underlies the differences that appear on the surface.

By doing these practices with care and interest, we will discover the wholeness and security that lies within us. Compared with the thoughts and moods that pass over the surface of the mind, that inner completeness is more real and lasting, and more truly our own.

What is Faith According to the Non-dual Teachings?

It is sometimes said that the non-dual teachings present a kind of theory, and that our meditations and other practices are like the experiments through which we may confirm for ourselves the truth of the non-dual hypothesis.

There is some validity in this view. It rightly recognises that on this path, each of us makes our own investigations and our own discoveries, and that rigid ideas about ultimate reality are an obstacle, not a solution.

Yet the parallels with physical theories and research are not complete. There are important differences. What are they?

In empirical research, both the theories and the evidence are distinct from the investigator, and the more the theories and the findings can be separated from the investigator's point of view, the better.

In contrast, non-duality in theory and practice is concerned with our ultimate Self, with what is not separate from the enquirer in any way. All separation is what we are seeking to overcome.

Another point is that the physical investigator is looking for empirical evidence which corresponds to the theory. The evidence and the theory are closely connected and both involve descriptions of the objective world. The non-dual teaching on the nature of our true Self, as was said, is also a kind of hypothesis, which has to be given in words and forms that the mind can grasp. But Self-realisation, or Enlightenment, completely transcends anything we may experience on the path; it does not resemble any kind of thought or sense experience. Direct knowledge of reality, the ultimate Self of all, is not mediated by the forms of thought, or the brain, or space or time. It is that in which all these appear.

One further difference between empirical investigation and the non-dual enquiry is that strong scientific support for a physical theory leads to further questions and new or refined hypotheses. In contrast, the ultimate Self-knowledge is absolute and final. Regarding the reality-status of the world and the nature of the Self, it leaves nothing further to be known, nor can it ever be lost.

So there is a gap, a radical divide, between investigation on the path to enlightenment and the final discovery, a gap which does not occur in the exploration of nature. This means that the final non-dual discovery cannot be shared directly; it does not fit any conventional form of thought and communication. Students of nature, given the required aptitude and perseverance, can in principle be led step by step from a rudimentary level to an understanding of the current theories. In the case of the non-dual enquiry, the teachings can indicate the way, but there is a point beyond which the senses and mind, and all knowledge that can be demonstrated publicly, cannot go.

In our scientific, technological world, there is a distrust of anything that is not supported by independent evidence. This is a healthy attitude in its right place. But it should be clear that if we seek rational and empirical demonstrations where reason and the senses do not apply, only confusions can result. Questions arise such as: Is the ultimate truth really there to be found? Is it worthy of our highest devotion and efforts? The answer is 'Yes', but the only way to 'prove' this is in direct experience, which cannot be shared publicly. Words cannot convey the magnitude of this truth. Here reassurance from an illumined source is the only guidance that can be offered.

There is a way to the realisation of this truth, which is open to all. It involves the cultivation of certain qualities of mind. One of these great life-skills and keys to liberation is called in Sanskrit *shraddha*.

This word shraddha is often translated as faith or trust, but those words do not express the full meaning, and may have some unhelpful associations. True shraddha grows from an understanding of what we have just been considering: in the non-dual enquiry there is a point beyond which there can be no complete explanations and public demonstrations. Only indications are possible. Shraddha is the inner balance, clarity and readiness to go on, in the light of higher guidance, to the goal of absolute inner freedom and illumination.

How do we develop shraddha? It is by using all our powers of observation and reason in the right way, up to their limit. We are offered guidance from an illumined source, then it is up to us to absorb what we have heard, and we do this by carefully thinking, and feeling, how it applies to us personally.

The non-dual philosophy explains how our human situation comes about so that we find ourselves to be apparently isolated individuals, vulnerable and mortal, within a vast cosmos. But it is possible to overcome this apparent separation and know the reality in us, free of limitations and suffering. Even at the beginning of our search, there is something in our immediate experience that is unchanging and self-luminous, and this is the opening that leads to joy and ultimately to transcendence.

It is for each of us to consider these teachings, and if we find them meaningful and satisfying, to assimilate and apply them. Every step forward involves a balance of theory and practice. In fact, as our investigations proceed, guidance and application merge, as we gain a heightened awareness of what is happening in our mind. Theory and practice fuse into a life of wise love and inner discovery, when it becomes our habit to dwell on the non-dual insights and affirmations, to the exclusion of unhelpful, obstructive thoughts.

Let us consider one of the challenges we are likely to meet on the path, and how we can overcome it. Put simply, it is that much of the time we have the strong feeling that we are our mind, and no more; that our thoughts and feelings, our joys and sufferings, are what we are. This conviction constantly challenges the teaching that we are much more than the mind, and are ultimately not bound by its limitations. And so we might find ourselves immobilised, half-consciously waiting and hoping for a solution to this problem which prevents us from progressing on the path.

But what would we be waiting for? Could it be for an intellectual proof of what cannot be proven intellectually, or an experience that can only come after, not before, we have taken the necessary steps? The solution to this lingering doubt cannot be the kind of proof that we might expect in a course of empirical investigation. At this point on the inner path what we need is shraddha.

It is true that we may be aware of the feeling 'I am my mind and affected by its ups and downs'.

Shraddha is the inner clarity and strength to recognise: 'Yes, that is how it feels, but I am more, much more, than any feeling. In my deeper nature I am the consciousness that reveals all thoughts and feelings, and is not limited by any of them.'

There is nothing naive or intellectually lazy about shraddha. It is a heightened awareness of what is happening in our mind, and of the true power of our own inner resources. Shraddha is the intuitive certainty that the reality in me is the reality underlying and transcending all limitations.

This conscious shraddha, free from all narrowness, can liberate us from deep-seated insecurities and inhibitions, opening the way to absolute freedom from all the bonds and limitations of time-space-causation.

Are My Ideas About the Supreme Being Important?

What is the aim of our study of the non-dual teachings? It is to expand our consciousness and to discover a fulfilment and security that nothing can disturb.

On this path, much depends on our beliefs about ourselves and the great whole of which we are a part. When we think about these questions and reflect on what the wisdom traditions tell us, we find ourselves considering what is sometimes called the supreme Being, or God. Whatever name, or names, we use, the deep-seated ideas we have about ultimate Reality affect our enquiries and meditation. So it is helpful to reflect on the non-dual teachings about the supreme power or principle, which religions call God and philosophers call the Absolute, and how these teachings can guide and support us on the way of inner discovery.

In non-duality, expressions, words or names equivalent to 'God' indicate the totality of all existence, the highest truth. Sometimes the name *Brahman* is used to refer to the supreme Reality, known from no particular point of view in time and space, but as the transcendental, absolute Truth. Brahman, or God, is the existence in everything that exists.

We have to be careful not to fall into confusion when we talk about this highest Truth. We cannot ask 'what came before time?' or 'where is space located?' Why not? Because such questions assume that the framework of time and space already exists. Similarly, there are many questions we cannot ask about God in the normal way. Can we say that God is the cause or creator of the world? We can only talk of causes when we divide things up and say that one thing led to another. If we think of the whole as being the totality of absolutely everything, obviously there are no real divisions, and so we cannot speak of causes or a creator.

Having said that, if we think of finite entities within the universe, including our body and mind, we can say that they have their support and origin in the absolute whole. So if we call the absolute 'God', then clearly, in this relative sense, that is the source and sustainer of all the individualities. This means that what we may refer to as God deserves the highest respect and gratitude. Yet we need to remember that no idea we have about this can be the complete and final truth. If we become rigid in our thinking, we may find ourselves dedicated, not to truth, but to a limited projection of our own mind.

One might say, 'Would it not be best then to leave aside all such talk and avoid any discussion about ultimate reality, whatever we may call that?' But this is not really an option. As thoughtful human beings we cannot say that the ultimate truth about everything is of no interest or importance. In order to think about what matters most and how to make the best of our lives, to hear and study teachings on wisdom, we need words, concepts and symbols.

For true seekers these questions are of particular interest, because an important step to deeper knowledge is the willingness to question everything we think we know about ourselves and the world around us. We may be surprised to find that however open-minded we consider ourselves to be, we do in fact harbour deeply-held convictions about the nature of things, convictions that go beyond the evidence and the scope of reason. If we learn to become aware of these limitations in our thinking, we open ourselves up to illumined guidance.

The non-dual teachings begin by inviting us to ask ourselves, what is our own current understanding of the highest truth? What do we think of as really real? The next step is to ask further, does this leave anything uncertain, anything unfulfilled? A true understanding of the nature of the supreme Reality, God, Brahman, whatever name we use, will resolve these questions: it is that which leaves nothing else to be known or done. This Reality can be verified in our own experience, for it is ever present. Without that presence nothing else could exist.

Where and how are we to seek? Clearly this supreme Being is not a fact or object like all the others we have come to know so far in life. It is unlike anything we have known, and is to be sought in a different way. Rather than exercising our mental faculties, the enquiry into ultimate truth means discerning in our inner experience what remains when all mental activity is brought to a profound tranquillity and our conscious awareness is focused one-pointedly on itself.

If God is the reality in all things, then God is the reality in us. To use the Sanskrit words, Atman (Self) is identical in essence with Brahman (God, the supreme Being). This teaching is essentially simple and logical, but so great in its implications that in practice we need authoritative guidance to advance from a theoretical understanding to direct experience.

Progress depends on regularly reminding ourselves about the truth of our own being. The goal of all our endeavours is to find our way back, so to say, to our ultimate home. Partly because it can be easily misunderstood, some wisdom traditions express this teaching only partially and indirectly. The non-dual philosophy presents it as directly as possible for the guidance of those who are willing to make the necessary efforts and adjustments to receive it without distortions.

As we saw, to absorb this higher teaching on God and Self, we first have to be willing to loosen our attachment to any limited conceptions of the supreme Being. This does not mean rejecting what is most valuable, even sacred, to us; it is to recognise that our intellect has limitations and that reality is infinitely greater than anything that our finite mind can conceive.

We may ask, is it possible to love God, if that is a name for what is so far beyond our understanding? The answer is not only that we can, but that in truth we have to, because it is one-pointed devotion that leads to the goal in all endeavours, and without love, our dedication will not be complete. This should not discourage us, because if something is necessary, it is possible.

God is truth absolute, and is also beauty absolute, so we cannot really love anything else because God is the essence of all. Therefore let us look beyond appearances and realise that the true object of our love in anyone or anything is that deeper reality that is one with our true Self.

There is a difference between love for objects and ideals, and loving another conscious being. In the non-dual philosophy God is Being Absolute, and is also Consciousness Absolute. The ultimate source of the consciousness in all beings, is the absolute consciousness of God. So love of God is not love of an inert object or abstraction. Through the non-dual practices we enquire, with alertness and precision, into what is truly our self, as opposed to the objects we experience. Similarly, we enquire into what is real in the world, as opposed to the appearances. When God is understood as the Reality in all, and the ultimate source of all consciousness, then the highest devotion and the highest metaphysical enquiry fuse into one quest for Self-knowledge and realisation.

It should not surprise us that the object of our highest love lies beyond what we can know in the ordinary way. Beauty always includes an element of mystery, and if we ever feel that we know everything there is to know about an object or person, the charm and fascination fade.

We might ask further, can this supreme Being help us, if its nature is so different from our own? Again the answer is not only that God can help, but that in fact only God can really help us, being the highest reality and the ultimate source of all power and sustenance. The teachings also show how we can make ourselves receptive. True help comes when we do what needs to be done as well as we can, with the feeling that everything comes from the supreme Reality and rests in that. When this becomes our way of thinking and doing, then, whatever happens outwardly, inwardly all is well with us.

As we have found, our beliefs about God, Brahman, or whatever name we use for ultimate Reality, are important. It is not possible to have no views, and what we do believe profoundly affects our highest potentials and the possibility of our finding fulfilment. We are invited to become more aware of these influences at work within our mind, and gradually to make adjustments according to the principle that there is not more than one Reality, and we are essentially That. Here we will find a response to our need for love, understanding and help from a power far greater than our individuality. Fulfilment is possible when we awaken to the truth that the reality we seek is ever present as the pure being and light which sustains and reveals all experience.

How Can I Find the Reality Behind Appearances?

In previous chapters we have thought about the place of trust and faith in the non-dual teachings, and the significance of our ideas about what has been called the supreme Being, Brahman or God. Now we can consider how to progress further towards the direct experience of Reality.

We noted that the Absolute is beyond the range of our mind. Reality is not divided up in space and time; it is a perfect oneness, and therefore cannot be the cause, or the effect, of anything else. In ultimate reality, there is no distinction between observer and observed, one who knows and what is known. As such, this highest Reality transcends the reach of our usual understanding. Any conception we can form falls short of the complete and final truth.

And yet, it is clear that the fragmentary aspect of total reality that we experience does somehow exist in and depend upon the greater Absolute whole. So in this sense, the supreme Being, or God, is the source and sustainer of our world, and is not far from us at all, but is the ground of our own being, so to say.

How are we to resolve this hiatus in our understanding of the highest truth? How can ultimate reality be apparently so far from us, and yet evidently so close? This question is at the root of philosophical enquiry. The intellect, as a detail of nature, cannot answer it. If that transcendent Truth is to be known, it will not be as a thought or theory in the mind. It can only be in the experience of non-separation. Such a direct experience of Truth as the essence of our own Being, is what is sometimes called enlightenment, that is, awakening to the essential nature of our own Self and realising its infinitude, perfection and freedom from all suffering and limitations. This is the goal of the non-dual teachings in theory and practice.

In our pursuit of higher knowledge, and a more fulfilling life generally, we need help and support. It has been asked, if and how the non-dual reality, God, understood in this way, can help us? As we saw, in principle the answer is simple: as the source and support of all things, only the supreme Being can really help us. The practical question is, what is necessary for us to be able to receive help?

Let us consider our own experience. When is it possible for us to give or receive any kind of help? The answer is, when there is trust. We have probably all experienced how if, for example, a child, or a newcomer, or colleague or friend, trusts us in some connection, then help can be offered. But where there is no trust, help is almost impossible. The same applies to our 'relation' with the universal Being that underlies our apparently individualised being. Trust is the key to deeper communion.

As we saw in chapter three, this trust is a kind of mental stability. Suppose we have reflected carefully and have come to understand that there is a deeper reality behind appearances. Suppose also we are convinced that to know this Reality is the highest good. It is then that we need not be swayed by distractions or easily diverted by random thoughts like, 'O, let's not bother', 'let's occupy ourselves with something easier'. When such thoughts arise, we have the stability and insight to reach out to what has been called our True Friend. This is trust.

When this trust is established, we can develop what is called 'skill in action'. In essence, this great life-skill means meeting all eventualities with equanimity, based on the conviction that everything comes to us as a teaching or revelation from that deeper Reality, our true Self. In turn, we learn to think of our actions as responses and offerings to that supreme power. When this is our way of living, our actions are liberating, truly creative, and everything can be a helper and stepping stone on the way to the goal of Self-realisation.

To cultivate this skill in liberating action requires dedication, and dedication is the practical expression of love. So how is it possible to love Truth, where Truth is understood as the supreme non-dual Being? Let us appreciate an important psychological principle. We love those who provide what we need. We love our parents, our children, our life-partners, even our heroes, as participants in the fulfilment of our deepest needs. At its most refined, this interconnectedness evolves into a sense of identity. The highest love is a feeling that one's own being is indistinguishable from the being of the beloved.

What is the deepest need that those we love help us to fulfil? It is for contentment and inner security that nothing can spoil, not even the approaching end of our life. Is there anything or anyone with whom we can entirely absorb our individuality into a whole that nothing can dissolve? The answer is yes, it is the ultimate Truth or God, understood as the name for the reality untouched by the passing of time. This is the being that underlies our being. In this we can melt our separateness into an everlasting completeness. This is where our deepest needs are fulfilled. To understand this principle will deepen our love of Truth, and love in turn will strengthen the dedication that allows us to go further.

Trust and devotion enable us to pursue our enquiry into the question, 'What am I, really? What is the true nature of my being, my Self? What is the Ocean in which I am a wave?'

As we found, the way to enlightenment is not to deny our human need for meaningful achievements and emotional security. It is to understand the root of our needs and how they can be fulfilled. As we saw, this begins with the recognition that our mind and senses present to us a partial and fragmentary experience of reality, and this hides from us the nature of truth.

Having reached this conviction we can develop an intelligent trust in the presence of a deeper reality beyond appearances. That trust matures into an intuitive recognition, when we learn to see everything that happens as teaching on the way, and to regard our actions as responses to that.

This leads to the fulfilment of our deepest need of all, for an inner security that not even death can undermine. It is to this that all our yearnings for worldly success and love are leading. This is the discovery that our apparently individualised being was never really separate from the omnipotent being beyond the limited appearances. In truth, the Self and the Beloved are one.

Does Non-duality Lead
to Special Powers?

According to the non-dual teachings, our true substance, our innermost Self, is not separate from the ultimate source of all, the supreme intelligence that underlies and pervades the entire world appearance. The path to inner illumination is a gradual awakening to this reality and a growing recognition that this is what we really are. And what is called Enlightenment is the dissolution of all the apparent separations from that supreme Being.

It might seem to follow that progress on the path to Self-realisation would be evidenced by signs of a great force at work in our lives and of a growing ability to draw upon that power according to our will. Does this mean that if we are pursuing the non-dual teachings, we might expect to see effects of this power in our situation, manifesting perhaps as material prosperity, influence and well-being on all levels? Should we expect a rise of uncommon capacities for creativity and benevolence, such as supra-mental sources of knowledge or the ability to heal trauma and remove suffering?

On the other hand, if no such developments are occurring in our life, does this mean that we are not making progress with the non-dual practices? If such extraordinary qualities are not becoming apparent within our scope, could it be that we are doing something wrong or have failed to grasp something essential?

Let us put our mind at rest about this. If we are doing the suggested practices and sincerely enquiring in the direction of non-duality, and yet do not seem to be gaining special capacities or qualities, this does not mean that we are doing something wrong or making no progress. To count ourselves as normal or ordinary does not mean that we do not or cannot grow towards inner illumination. In fact, to be a normal person with an ordinary life, and no wish to appear otherwise, is an ideal situation in which to make the subtle, but vital, changes which constitute real progress on the inner quest.

What are those vital changes? At the core of all our life experience there is the awareness of 'I am'. This conscious principle is always with us, as the central point that our inner world revolves around. It is familiar to us, although imperfectly understood, and it is often called the ego.

This word 'ego' has become associated with exaggerated self-centeredness and self- importance. In fact, the ego is not intrinsically bad. If we did not have this fundamental core of 'I am' and 'I care', then the essence of our humanity would be missing. What matters is what this 'I-am' feeling is associated with—what we identify as our central 'I-am' or ego-sense.

At one stage in our development we are ruled by the conviction: 'I am my wants and my ideas, and everything else either helps me or gets in the way, or just doesn't matter!' This feeling, too, has its place. During this phase, we learn important lessons which gradually teach us that narrow self-interest is not an asset but a source of conflict and frustration around and within us.

In the light of these lessons, our identity-feeling gradually widens, becoming less focused on what is exclusive, and more on what is shared by all. This progression towards universality eventually leads us to take up the conscious enquiry into the nature of our true being, and this search culminates in the realisation that the 'I-am' in me is, in essence, that which reveals all experience. I am the living light in all conscious beings.

When used in this sense, the word 'I' indicates what is beyond all distinctions. It is what underlies and transcends everything finite, where there is no separation, no limitation, no suffering, and no possibility of suffering. This is the ultimate truth of our being, what is most correctly called our Self, now and always. The aim of our practices and inner enquiry is to discover this supreme fact in our own direct experience.

What then is the place of our body and mind with all their obvious limitations? The body and mind are precious because they sustain the life through which we may make this sublime discovery. The unique value of the human mind is that it can achieve a kind of transparency through which we realise with certainty that the mind is not the ultimate Self. The mind is precious because it is potentially the doorway to the realisation of the Absolute Being in which it appears to abide.

In the light of this supreme potentiality, we do not need to look for special powers in the belief that they might lead to fulfilment and happiness. The reality, the ultimate power, is our true being, and is infinite.

The path to Self-knowledge, then, is a return to true normality. Our meditations and other practices help us to uncover the unspoilt quality of our inner nature, beneath the apparent disturbances that seem to obscure it.

Among these disturbances is mental tension. We may have become so accustomed to living with this internal pressure that it feels normal and almost inevitable. Some tension is appropriate sometimes, but even in our modern life, those moments are passing, not continuous. What perpetuates tension is an underlying insecurity. The non-dual teachings point to the root of that insecurity and tension, and how they can be resolved through meditation based on a deeper self-understanding, revealing a natural state of balanced relaxation.

The practices also help us to break the habit of being lost in an endless series of mental associations and distractions. This habitual condition has been called 'the stream of consciousness', although it would be better called the stream of unconsciousness.

To many of us, the first thing that happens when we try to meditate is that we become aware of how uncontrolled our thoughts are and how difficult it is to concentrate on something we have consciously chosen. Realising this, it might seem that meditation is making us feel worse rather than better. But to become aware of this state of affairs in our mind, even partially, is to unlock a powerful secret. It clearly reveals that our thoughts are not our Self, and that our true identity lies elsewhere. Then, even if the uncontrolled thoughts do not entirely cease, their relative insignificance is exposed. If we persevere with our meditation practice, the awareness underlying thoughts increasingly shines through, revealing more about our deeper nature than any textbook ever could, and illuminating the way forward to yet deeper discoveries.

Thus, by providing an antidote to our tension and distraction, the practices can prevent us from dissipating mental energy uselessly, opening up reserves of resilience and vitality. Is this not in itself a rather special power?

We can overcome many obstacles to well-being on all levels if we are able to feel happiness in the happiness of others, even those who might seem to be better placed than us individually. Through our practice and enquiry we realise that our true I-am is the light of pure consciousness, deeper than personality, and at this fundamental level, we are one with all. When we recognise this, dark clouds are dispelled and our inner environment becomes naturally sunny.

Progress on the path, then, is more of an unburdening and letting go than any kind of acquisition.

There is one form of letting go which is especially significant. In some of the classical writings of the non-dual tradition, it is said that one sure manifestation of real progress is a growing perception that the world as we experience it through our mind and senses, is not entirely real.

This teaching is subtle and has to be rightly understood. It is never helpful to be careless in our dealings with the world. Let us always fulfil our responsibilities and care for those around us, as well as we can.

What this teaching about the apparently illusory nature of the world really means, is that we become increasingly convinced that we will not find lasting fulfilment and security in the world revealed to us through our senses. This is because nothing that is limited can truly be connected with the limitless Reality of our own being. Only the immortal can satisfy the immortal in us. Only the infinite can satisfy the infinite in us.

This growing conviction shows that we are being freed of deep-seated attachments to external things—things that will pass sooner or later. We are gaining a new independence, deep in our own heart, at the well-spring of our thoughts and feelings.

A developing awareness that the phenomenal world known through the mind lacks something essential may also be a challenging stage on our journey. It might lead to feelings of despondency and depression, unless it is balanced by positive intimations that our ultimate goal is attainable.

How is that ultimate goal to be attained? There is an innate yearning in every human heart to be totally free of all constraints and limitations. Our mind is constantly trying to find solutions to our difficulties, and so it may imagine the acquisition of special powers as the key to liberation and fulfilment. But the real means to liberation is the higher Self-knowledge.

It is not powers generated in our body and mind that will bring relief. Freedom comes with the knowledge that our real Self does not need special powers to rise above the limitations of mundane life, because our true nature does not need anything at all, and never could be in any need, being ever absolute and perfect.

Self-realisation is not something that our will-power can ever bring about. It is revealed when the inner conditions are right. What we can do is to cultivate those conditions, and every step we take in this direction is at the same time an unburdening and inner expansion, right now.

It might seem counter-intuitive to say that a vital step forward is to fully understand that nothing within the range of our imagination will bring us complete happiness and ultimate fulfilment. But is it not a relief to realise that we do not have to struggle to find fulfilment where it does not exist?

What we are recognising is that the world we experience through our mind is not a complete or accurate picture of reality. The more clearly we realise this, the more certain we become that there is a deeper reality behind that picture. That reality seems to be hidden, but it is closer than close. It is our own ever-present Self.

What is the Relation Between Thought and Awareness?

One of the central points considered in the non-dual teachings, is that there is a difference between thought and awareness, between everything in our mind, and our awareness of it.

Thoughts are passing and finite: each thought has its particular form and qualities and is rapidly succeeded by another. In contrast, awareness is unchanging; it reveals equally everything that passes through the mind. In awareness we find no gaps or boundaries. We experience the one awareness, making all experience possible.

A particularly significant difference is that thoughts depend on awareness to reveal them, but awareness itself depends on nothing else to reveal it. Awareness is its own light. Conscious awareness is uniquely self-sufficient in this way.

It follows that we do not have to be limited by the feeling 'I am my thoughts and feelings, and no more'. By deepening the sense that we are our awareness, we may discover a new dimension of inner freedom and fulfilment.

Having heard these teachings, the next step is to investigate them for ourselves. Looking within, we can confirm the vital distinction between thoughts and feelings, and the awareness of them. In doing so, we see a way opening up from mental constriction towards inner expansion and independence, leading to the realisation that the consciousness illuminating our life from within is in essence identical with the light of universal consciousness, immaculate and infinite.

It is important that we do not just accept theories without making efforts to verify them for ourselves. And if we sincerely pursue this enquiry, we may expect to encounter challenges on the way.

One such challenge might present itself like this. We may decide: 'Now I am going to explore the difference between thoughts and awareness, by simply watching my thoughts as a detached observer.'

But then an inner voice might say, 'Isn't that just another thought? "I am the one watching my thoughts", seems to be one more thought, does it not?' If we notice or detect the occurrence of a thought in the mind, that 'noticing' or 'detecting' forms more thought. And if we do not notice or detect in any way thoughts coming and going, then we are not being aware of the mind. It seems that whatever position we take in relation to the mind and its thoughts, that is another mental process, one more thought.

As a result, we may conclude that this investigation cannot lead to the discovery of anything essentially different from thought, any more than a river could be detached from its own flow.

And another question arises. If we are carefully reflecting, we may ask: 'What exactly do we mean by awareness?' In order to distinguish awareness from what it is not, to identify with it, and to deepen this experience, we must be able to think about awareness, to compare it with what is not aware, to reflect on it in various ways. In that case, how can we say that awareness is essentially different from all the other ideas that occur in the mind? If we consider and investigate awareness, then it is an object that we have become aware of, not awareness itself.

And so it would seem that any endeavour to know more fully the nature of awareness is futile and self-defeating. But if we cannot observe or understand awareness in some way, then awareness amounts to nothing in our experience; the word has no meaning.

We began with the teaching that there is an essential difference between thought and awareness. But going into this we have found apparent contradictions and no clear solutions. Should we conclude that there is not a real distinction between the contents of the mind and our conscious awareness? If so, there would seem to be no possibility of finding any freedom and illumination beyond the boundaries of the finite mind.

Is there a way forward? First, let us notice that the mind has many aspects and levels. For example, there is one part of our mind which responds immediately to events. In some situations, an immediate reaction is appropriate, perhaps to avoid danger or damage. Then there is another phase of the mind which is able to observe and reflect on those reactions. And those reflections may themselves be further considered and refined. In this way we move, as it were, between levels of our mind according to the need of the moment.

All this evidently involves different levels and types of thought. And illuminating every phase is awareness itself, one consciousness that reveals equally the multitude of thoughts and mental activities. We can consider one aspect of the mind from another, and so we may progress from instinctive to reflective living. What thought cannot do is rise above itself altogether into the state of pure awareness.

Perhaps we have heard and understood this before. And yet, do we not sometimes find the mind trying to take the impossible step beyond itself, and seeming to fail, and wondering if there is something wrong with the teachings?

Does this throw light on our earlier difficulties? We are presented with the principle that there is an essential difference between thought and awareness. We proceed to investigate this and find that every attempt to simply observe thoughts, turns out to be just another thought. And so we wonder if the teachings are mistaken. In fact, what is happening is that our thought is trying to place itself above thought, and inevitably, cannot.

This is an important lesson for the mind about its own role and limits. Sometimes as a form of meditation practice, we do try to simply observe our thoughts as a detached witness. We can learn and benefit much from this practice. But it is not meant to put the mind itself into the position of pure awareness.

What then is the true relation between thought and awareness?

At the unillumined stage of our life we do not know our own true Self, but it is possible to discover our true Self in direct experience. This revelation is called Enlightenment, and in knowing our true Self, we know the Self of all, the universal Reality, and thus find release from all limitations and suffering.

The nature of the ultimate Self cannot be expressed in words, but it may be indicated provisionally as pure conscious awareness. It follows that our true Self is not our mind, and that the Self is to be discovered by turning in the direction of our own awareness.

The teaching that our mind is not our true Self is contrary to the compelling feeling that we are our mind, that the mind's ups and downs and limitations are our own. We can overcome the conviction that we are the mind and nothing more by reflecting on the essential differences between the many, changing, limited qualities of what we experience, and the pure, self-luminous, unchanging consciousness that illumines all experience.

So this teaching on the distinction between the contents of experience and our awareness is a helpful step. But it is not the highest truth.

We may have already asked ourselves, how can there be a complete separation between thought and awareness, between mind and consciousness? Does that not contradict the principle of non-duality, that ultimate reality is undivided? If consciousness and objects are entirely different, how can there be any interaction between them? How can pure infinite unchanging consciousness have any connection with ever-changing, limited experiences? How is our awareness of thoughts possible if they are two entirely distinct principles?

Up to this point we have been thinking of conscious awareness as comparable to an inner light or observer, shining or looking on all experiences equally and not constrained by any of them. This is a helpful idea while we are trying to understand that we are more than the mind and not limited by it.

But the idea of conscious awareness, Self, as a light and witness is not the final truth. It is more completely true to say that pure consciousness is the underlying nature, the essential being of which all phenomena are formed. It does not illuminate objects and experiences from outside; it is their essence and substance, as it were.

To use an analogy that is far from perfect, consciousness is not so much like a light revealing phenomena; it is more like the universal energy of which all things are formed. But this analogy should not be pushed too far, because the true Self is consciousness absolute and no limitations in space and time or causation apply to it.

The practice of stepping back from thoughts and identifying with awareness is a helpful one up to a point, but it is not sufficient to lead us to the highest truth. Progress depends on a balance of two elements, theory and practice. The theory is conveyed through the teachings that we receive as guidance from an illumined source. They point us towards the truth that surpasses anything the mind could conceive or discover unaided. The practice is to reflect and meditate on what is indicated by that illumined source.

It is correct that there is an essential distinction between all limited phenomena, mental and physical, and the true Self, which may be indicated as universal consciousness. But it is not just the difference between observer and observed.

All one can say is that Self is absolutely real, and everything else is not absolutely real. Phenomena abide in absolute consciousness, but absolute consciousness is not limited by the phenomena, which do not share its absolute reality. Our true nature, our I, is the absolute reality. On enlightenment, the Self is realised, and the status of phenomena is exposed. Words can go no further.

Can There Be a Name
for the Nameless?

The non-dual teachings give us the explanations and guidance we need on the path to self-realisation. They show where our difficulties come from, and provide solutions. The teachings acknowledge that our body and mind will always be affected by the ups and downs of life. This is why nothing in the world seems to entirely fulfil us, and we are never completely free of anxiety. Yet we also learn from the teachings that our body and mind exist within a greater whole, which encompasses and transcends all the changes. Our true nature is at one with that greater whole.

The feeling that we are our body and mind and no more, is the outcome of a distorted or incomplete view, which may be overcome through direct Self-knowledge. Here lies the possibility of freedom from all limitations, suffering and uncertainty. This freedom is also our natural condition. The path to inner illumination is a journey home, not to a distant land, and the teachings offer practical guidance on how to approach this discovery for ourselves.

What is the essential first step towards this inner awakening? It is to bring harmony and stability into our mind and our relationships with those around us, through ethical and considerate living. This stage is shared by all the genuine wisdom traditions, and the guidance is for everyone.

Then, if we choose, we may pursue the highest fulfilment by embarking on an inner enquiry into the nature of our own being. We learn to distinguish between appearance and reality, self and not-self, what passes and what abides eternally.

In this endeavour, meditation and related practices are central, supported by reflection on the philosophy, and the on-going ethical living, which conduces to inner integrity and affirms our connectedness with all creatures.

One of the practical challenges we face is how to keep all this in focus. We need a way to grasp the essentials and hold on to them. As we go about our life, at each moment, various aspects of the teachings will be relevant. We need a way of remembering what we have learned, so that it can infuse our mental world and guide our actions.

This is the challenge of how to live consciously, and all the wisdom traditions recognise and respond to it. They offer representations of Truth, tangible or abstract, that we can keep in mind and connect with as a living presence. Such teachings also provide ways of expressing reverence or appeals for support, that can be made vocally or inwardly.

A concentrated form of this practice is to take a name of what is highest and to repeat it, outwardly or inwardly, whenever we need help in sustaining our re-membrance of the deeper truth. Any meaningful name may be used in this way. Among them are Buddha, Allah, God, Rama, Krishna, Christ or Brahman—a word indicating the Absolute, the Whole. Alterna-tively—or in addition—we may feel an affinity with words or names such as Light, Truth, Beauty Absolute.

To repeat such a word or name to ourselves will not take us away from the present situation or distract us from coping with it. Such a name will always help us, because the effect is to focus the mind on what is real and important to us and needs attention right now. The name will awaken associations that are supportive and creative.

We can more fully understand the power of names of truth if we observe certain features of the way our mind works.

A significant fact is that we can only think about one thing at a time. This is concealed by the way the mind moves swiftly from one idea to another. But even when we are 'multi-tasking', our attention is actually switching rapidly between subjects, and at any moment it is occupied with just one of them.

This characteristic of our thinking process is the key to effective psychological self-help. It means that by replacing one thought with another, we make a real difference to the condition of our mind. And with practice, it is possible to replace the stream of random and disconnected ideas, with one sustained idea or a sequence of consciously directed thoughts.

The power to select and focus on particular thoughts or ideas is the basis of meditation and it is the way we may pass through the appearances and distractions on the surface of our mind, to the deeper level of our being, which is not isolated from the reality in all, and where lasting security and fulfilment are to be found.

If we can only think of one thing at a time, we might wonder how we can have the complex mental life that we do. Part of the answer relates to another feature of the mind, which is the way it forms concepts.

With extreme facility, our mind puts ideas and impressions together into single compounds. Concepts we use all the time, like 'friend' or 'holiday' or 'home', are composed of so many impressions and associations, that if we analysed them completely, they would each fill a book. But once these concepts are formed, our mind can take each of them as one idea, and then merge or combine them with others.

Forming concepts in this way is so natural to us that we hardly notice it happening, but without this ability our human experience would be unrecognisable.

We can now understand why the practice of re-peatedly recalling a name of the highest truth is so powerful: it is because our thought-space is occupied by the name to the exclusion of other ideas, and the name carries a distillation of meaning and a wealth of associations.

Among all the names for higher Truth, one has been the chosen focus for many students of non-duality, and that is OM.

In recent times, OM has been widely popularised, even commercialised, but if we put aside any precon-ceptions, we can find its true significance and value for us.

OM is presented in the Upanishads, but it belongs to no particular language or religion. Its full meaning is elucidated by the non-dual teachings. It can thus be used by those who identify with any wisdom tradition or none. OM signifies the supreme Reality, the source of all. It includes all levels of experience, and bridges the divide between experience and the one who experiences.

OM indicates non-duality in a particular way. In most cases, an object and its name are distinct, and many different names could be and sometimes are used for the same object. In the case of OM, the name and the named are not separable in this way.

OM is sometimes written as the three letters AUM, corresponding to the sounds of which it is comprised and the levels of symbolic meaning. When pronounced aloud, AUM begins with the sound A, then comes U and finally M: A-U-M. This includes all the open vowel sounds. All the other sounds are made by restricting or stopping these vowels. So OM includes in essence all the sounds that all names are formed of, as well as being a name for the All and the source of All.

The phases of AUM are related to levels of our experience. Each day our life comprises a regular cycle and combination of three states of consciousness, which may be called the waking state, the dreaming state and deep sleep.

In the waking state we mostly experience the world around us through our senses. In dreams, it is our mind that manufactures the forms we experience. In deep sleep, there is no experience of objects, but all our cognitive powers are latent, ready to be brought back into operation.

The three states are interconnected. During the waking state, although our senses predominate, our mind is actively organising the sense-data and projecting memories and associations onto what we perceive. In the dream state, many of the impressions received when awake are still active. And in deep sleep, although there is no subject-object awareness, all our mental faculties remain as potentialities, and on waking after deep sleep, we often find that somewhere outside the range of our awareness, connections have been made in our understanding, and things put into better perspective.

In AUM, the first sound, represented by A and pronounced 'Ah', symbolises the receptive level of the mind, where the senses predominate, as they do while we are awake. 'Ah' is a natural sound and one that is often associated with new experiences: 'Ah, what's this?'

The second part, written as U and sounding like 'Oh', indicates the internal working of the mind, which composes pictures out of the sense-impressions and memories, and is most obviously at work in the dream state. Again it is a natural sound, often expressive of mentally putting things together: 'Oh, I see.'

Finally, M indicates the withdrawal of the mental powers, which nonetheless remain latent and ready to be revived by new stimuli. Once again, this is a natural sound, associated with conclusion and satisfaction: 'Mmm...'

When AUM is repeated, between each repetition there comes a silence. Silence is the medium in which sounds occur, and this silence is revealed whenever sound is absent. The silence between repetitions of OM relates to what underlies all three phases of mental life, and that is pure conscious awareness.

Pure consciousness is present equally in the waking, dreaming and deep sleep states, which seem to obscure it, but could not exist without it. And at the universal level, pure consciousness is the ultimate reality, whose names include Brahman, God, the Absolute and OM.

 OM is also represented visually. It is comprised of three curves, symbolising the waking, dreaming and deep sleep states. Above them is a point of no dimensions, representing the pure consciousness which has no limitations. Between the three curves and the point is part of a circle standing for infinity.

In one sense, the point is closest to the state of mental quiescence (3), but at the same time it is that which reveals and makes possible all the states.

OM, then, is a name for ultimate Truth, the Truth behind all our experiences. As such, it is the object of our highest love, reverence and aspirations. By repeating the name OM, we can keep the essential teachings in the background—or the foreground—of our mind. Remembrance of OM replaces unwanted thoughts, focuses the attention on what is really important, and sets off the most helpful associations. To concentrate our thoughts on OM arouses the highest love. To repeat OM with feeling, fills the understanding with light.

Because the name and the named are at one in OM, repeating OM helps us pass on from thinking about the teachings to becoming absorbed in what they indicate, and ultimately identified with that. Seekers and devotees have found that practices based on OM are an effective way of bringing the theory to life in our own being.

As with all names that denote the highest reality, we may call on OM spontaneously, whenever we need immediate help. We can make a practice of repeating OM at certain times. And we may find that the repetition of OM becomes almost as natural and continuous as our breathing and forms a foundation of our inner quest.

OM may also have a place in the special time we dedicate each day to meditation. Here are two practices that could be included in a structured meditation session similar to those presented in other chapters of this book.

Breathing Practice

Breathe consciously, deeply, evenly, making the in and out-breath the same length. If possible breathe through the nose. Then, as you breathe in, hear inwardly the sound 'O', and on the out-breath, hear the sound 'M'. Relax deeply by focusing your attention on the sound 'O' as you breathe in fully; hearing the sound 'M', let go of all tension as you breathe out completely.

While doing this practice there is no need to think about the meaning of OM. For now we are using it to practise making the mind still and focused; helpful associations will naturally follow. Whenever the mind wanders, as soon as you notice, bring the attention back to your breath, and O-M. Do this for the time you have chosen.

Visualisation

For a few moments, look at the visual form of OM. Do not strain in any way, just look at OM, as you would look at a painting. Then close your eyes and see OM inwardly as if drawn in light. Keep your attention on the form of OM in light.

Let your thoughts be about the way the form of OM represents the states of consciousness, and what underlies them all. In this way, keep the image of OM steadily before your inner eye for the chosen time.

OM is a name and the named. It is a signpost and the destination. If we call upon it, OM will prove to be an inner support at every stage on our way to realisation of the one without a second.

Seeking Happiness, Should I Pursue or Give Up Desires?

As enquirers into the highest human potentialities, we may feel that we are being presented with a choice: whether, in the pursuit of happiness, it is best to wholeheartedly try to get what we want, or, to practise giving up desires, which seems to be the example set by some of the great teachers of humanity. Let us consider this question from the non-dual perspective.

The first thing to be clear about is that happiness is the goal. We are meant to be happy. To be a really happy person is a great and perhaps rare, human achievement. Our pursuit of happiness is sometimes inhibited by fear of failure. But there are good reasons why we can and should be truly ambitious when it comes to happiness. And the outcome is very much in our own hands.

The second point to recognise is that it is natural and inevitable for us to have desires. At the root of all desires is that fundamental desire for happiness and well-being. To be entirely free of desires while living in this world is neither realistic nor necessary.

So is there anything fundamentally wrong with desire? It is only that to have a desire implies that we are not yet fully happy, that in some way we feel incomplete and lacking. The ultimate message of the non-dual teachings, and the root of all authentic wisdom traditions, is that in our true nature we are not incomplete or wanting in any way, and in fact never have been. Our highest Self is, in truth, at one with the supreme Being, perfect, invulnerable, beyond all limitations and suffering.

Even the desire to realise this truth of our own nature is in a sense misplaced, as it arises from the conviction that we are somehow separated from that Truth, and this starting point is ultimately a distorted view. It is in this sense that all desire is based on a profound misconception, which can be dispelled through deeper self-knowledge.

This is the standpoint of those who have awakened to the highest Reality—the view, so to speak, from the summit of wisdom. Still, the non-dual teachings recognise that for many of us, most of the time, our actual experience is of being much affected and limited by all the joys and sorrows, well-being and hardship, that the mind and body are exposed to. When this is where we find ourselves, it may seem that we are indeed presented with that choice: whether our best chance of finding happiness is through pursuing the satisfaction of immediate, tangible wants, or, by exercising self-restraint and endurance in pursuit of the final, but apparently distant, goal of inner illumination.

We do have to make choices and decisions, and choosing one thing may mean letting go of another. Yet learning how to be happy in the here and now is an essential part of the path to enlightenment, not an alternative to it. The teachings do not just tell us that we have to learn to be content and cheerful amidst the flux of life; they provide practical help and guidance.

First, we are encouraged to ask ourselves: 'What is happiness? What makes me happy?' It may be said provisionally that there are three forms or sources of happiness: the happiness associated with having;

happiness connected with doing; and happiness related to being.

It is certain that one kind of happiness is what we feel when we have something we really like. Most intense is how we feel at the moment of getting what we want. We are all familiar with this kind of experience. We also know that such happiness tends to pass quickly. Clearly, this kind of happiness includes not getting what we do not want. Again, we feel this most keenly at those moments when we are relieved of adversity.

Secondly, there is happiness connected with doing. The quality of our life depends much on the sense that we are engaged in useful activity. This may come simply with being in a situation which we like, so that is really just another case of getting what we want. But that is not always so. Sometimes there is a real sense of happiness arising from the knowledge that we are doing the right thing in the right way. This kind of happiness is clearly distinct from simply getting what we like, and can affect us deeply, so we have to include this in our consideration of what is happiness.

Finally comes what we called the happiness of being. If we are seriously interested in these teachings, we have already begun to perceive that true happiness is not something we gain from outside, nor is it something we become. True happiness, joy—in Sanskrit, *ānandam*—is intrinsic to our nature. It cannot come or go, or increase or decrease, and, as such, it is free of all fear, which is why it is the greatest happiness. This can be confirmed in direct experience.

In the light of these teachings, we will see that daily life provides many intimations and indications of where true happiness lies. It is a partial glimpse of this happiness that makes deep sleep so sweet. The happiness of knowing that we are doing the right thing is the feeling of harmony with the reality in our own being and in all beings. And increasingly we will realise that even the happiness of getting what we want does not arise from the object but in the momentary freedom from want that occurs at the instant the desired object is achieved. It is this pause in the mental activity that gives us the sense of completeness and self-sufficiency which is our true nature.

What we have called happiness then, in truth, always arises from a realisation of our own Being. Our passing and partial experiences of happiness are a brief thinning of the fog of irrelevant and distracting mental activity that seems to cut us off from what we really are.

How then are we to make this experience complete and perfect, while addressing and balancing all the competing demands of life? It is not by trying to fulfil all desires, or to give up desire completely, but by overcoming our sense of limitation and the anxiety that springs from it.

Let us try to understand our situation. The real reason we cannot give up desires is because we cannot give up doing. Our body and mind belong to this world of time, space, matter and energy, so we find ourselves inextricably being and doing amidst this flux. As conscious human beings, there is always some choice in what we do, and we act according to a range of motives, at the root of which is the fundamental desire to be happy and avoid suffering. So giving up desire completely is no more possible than getting out of time and space and this changing world.

What we need is a way of finding happiness amidst this flow of being and doing. And what usually prevents us from finding it, is uncertainty and anxiety about what is going to happen. How does this come about? Typically, we make efforts and act with the aim of achieving some goal or result, and we feel that our well-being is dependent on that result. Anxiety is introduced because of uncertainty about the outcome, and unhappiness arises if it is not as we wished.

How are we to free ourselves from these self-imposed limitations? The first step is to live fully in the present. Every instant is new. Thinking or worrying about what we did a moment ago, and what might come of it, only distracts us from what matters in this present moment. If something has been set in motion and it is time to turn to another task, then let us be focused on that. We can convince and remind ourselves that this is the best way of being and doing, and it will relieve us of much anxiety and tension.

As our understanding of non-duality deepens through our ongoing enquiry and meditation, there is a further step we can take, which leads through the present moment to the realm of timeless truth. The best we can do with our attachment and concern about the results of actions is to give them up, in the highest sense. We can recognise the fact that it is not in our power to control the outcome of events, and consciously leave it to the power that does underlie all happenings.

To put it another way, we can think of our efforts and actions as offerings to Truth, to the supreme Reality in us and in all. And when something is offered to That, we let go of our attachment and anxiety about it. In this way, what was a psychological burden is turned into a liberating affirmation.

This giving or offering up, is not to a distant authority, but to the reality at the heart of our own being. By making our life a flow of action as self-giving, we can acknowledge the full force of all the desires at work in our being: the fundamental will to be free of limitations and suffering, and all the subsidiary forms that takes. We can act wholeheartedly according to what we feel is for the best. When we leave the results of our actions to the power that does in truth support all that comes into being, we can find happiness and freedom in the here and now. It is by our actions above all that we affirm our growing realisation that the experience of separation belongs to the level of appearances and that our true Self is the universal Self of all beings.

How Can I Enquire Into
What is Beyond the Mind?

In pursuit of inner illumination, alongside meditation and other practices, we are advised to study
and reflect on the philosophy of non-duality. At this
point we might say: 'I have heard that the deeper
truth necessarily lies beyond what can be expressed
in words and thoughts, so how can I think about
what is beyond thought? And why should I even try?'

It is true that our mind and thoughts are
necessarily occupied with qualities and quantities,
differences and connections, while ultimate reality
cannot be framed by time or space or characteristics
that belong to some objects and not to others. This
does seem to imply that it would be fruitless to think
about the truth beyond thought and that any attempt
to do so would be misguided.

And yet, how can we not think about what is
ultimately real? The will to know is intrinsic to our

human nature: the curiosity of children, the investigations of scholars and researchers, the reflections prompted by the approaching end of our lives, are all expressions of the fundamental human urge to know. Eventually, our thoughts are led towards the ultimate source and support of everything we experience. Until that is known, all knowledge is tentative and incomplete.

The non-dual teachings acknowledge the validity of both these apparently incompatible conclusions. Ultimate truth is beyond thoughts and words, yet truth can be known, not through words and thoughts, but by uncovering the ground of being on which all experience occurs. And progress on the path to that discovery depends on making the right use of our capacity for rational thinking and creative imagination.

True knowledge has to be uncovered from within; it cannot be infused by any power outside ourselves. In fact, the path is a process of enquiry—called in Sanskrit *vichara*—into the truth of our own being and, by extension, all being. All the other practices, including meditation, are ways of preparing the mind to pursue this end.

This enquiry is essential because the main challenge on the path, what stands between us and the lasting fulfilment of inner illumination, is what might be called a kind of 'not-knowing' or 'ignorance', to use that word in an entirely non-judgmental sense. Sometimes, the human condition at the beginning of our inner development is thought to be somehow innately at fault, or exiled, or caught in cycles of limitation. The non-dual view is that there is something essential that we do not yet know, which we have come into the world to discover. It follows that if the problem is not-knowing, then the solution is knowledge. Only knowledge can overcome ignorance, so knowledge is the goal. And the way to the goal of knowledge is a life of enquiry, the practice of vichara.

There are two aspects to our not-knowing. One is that we do not know our own true nature. Our true Self, our essential I, is somehow hidden from us. When it is fully known, our Self is revealed as not different in essence from the universal Self of all, and the feeling of incompleteness and insecurity is resolved forever. Secondly, as well as not knowing our true Self, we have a mistaken idea that we are something we are not: there is a compelling sense that we are the body and mind and no more, and that the limits and travails of the mind are our own. The mind-body is what we experience, and what we experience is not what we are in our true nature. Our Self is that which reveals the experiences and ever abides in its own perfection, self-luminous and self-sufficient.

Our task, then, is to resolve not-knowing by knowledge, that is, to overcome the impression that we are the body-mind and no more, and to open up the way to the realisation of our true self. All our inner faculties—our reason, our attention, imagination, memory, our focused emotions—are to be engaged in the life of enquiry, which is, initially, an enquiry into what Self is not. This is also a way of discovering what ultimate reality is not. It will become apparent that our own Self and the supreme Being, are not finite or limited in any way. As this truth becomes clearer, so too will the positive implication that our real Self is beyond limitations and imperfections, and is already present as the ground of our experience. A new light begins to illumine our inner world and the way ahead.

From what we have said so far it is clear that although the mind has a finite range and cannot encompass the ultimate truth, it is far from valueless. Indeed the human mind has a supreme value, which stems from its ability to recognise its own limits, and thus, by implication, that reality lies beyond itself. By acknowledging the limitations of the mind, we are beginning to take our stand on what transcends the mind.

We have been led to the logical conclusion, or intuitive feeling, that our true nature is not limited by the body and mind. Can the teachings go further than elucidating what we are not, and point positively to the truth of our being, the reality in all? The nature of the Self cannot be expressed in words, but the teachings can reassure us that the truth is there to be found, and indicate the direction in which it is to be sought. There is a reality beyond appearances, that is not bound by any limitations, and this reality is not distant from us: it is the essence of our life and consciousness.

Let us note that the non-dual philosophy does not try to prove this intellectually. Logic only establishes what may be inferred from a premise. We use reason to help us understand provisionally what self is not. Study of the philosophy will show that its conclusions are reasonable, but whether they are true or not can only be confirmed by direct experience. The teachings are given to us on the authority of those who have made the great discovery, and they are offered as encouragement and guidance for our own enquiry, if we choose to pursue it.

How then can we progress our own enquiry into the truth at the core of our being, where all apparent divisions are resolved? In other fields of study, progress is measured in the accumulation of facts and problem-solving skills. The aim of our metaphysical vichara is to bring about an inner change, such that all our thoughts and feelings are in harmony with the principles of non-duality and conduce to self-discovery.

Our progressive enquiry means first listening to, or reading about, the teachings from a reliable source. Really listening, without preconceptions, is an art, which takes practice. Then our task is to make the essential ideas our own—to find our own way of expressing them to ourselves in our own words, using our imagination. Let us be sure that we can do this. For example, the truth of non-duality follows from the principle that all individuation exists within a whole and that separations only appear when viewed from a particular perspective. We might think about this with an analogy from nature such as the way in which individual waves are not essentially different from the ocean. Similarly, the non-dual teachings point out that the inner light of conscious awareness requires no other light to reveal it: we can understand this idea and its significance by reflecting on our experience of physical light. In such ways, each of us can vitalise and make our own any other insight from the teachings that captures our attention.

Equally, it is for each of us to note where our thinking leads to doubts or apparent contradictions, and then to consider the solutions offered by the non-dual philosophy. How, we might wonder, can ultimate Reality be both the source and sustainer of the world, and beyond all change and limitation? How is it that pure consciousness and physical phenomena are entirely dissimilar and yet apparently interwoven in the lives of all sentient creatures? Could a supreme power or Being, that transcends space and time, be in any way concerned with our human situation? Is there any way for us to draw support and comfort from a principle so far beyond the adequacy of our thoughts and feelings?

The questions that arise and the form they take will vary for each of us, yet the non-dual philosophy provides guidance for us all. At the heart of the teachings is the distinction between appearances mediated by our mind, and the undivided reality beyond all limited perspectives. Our body and mind live in the world of phenomenal appearances, yet our innermost Self is ever identical with Brahman, the Real.

There seems to be a fundamental divide between our life in the world and the true Self of all. But this duality is itself apparent, not absolute. Phenomenal forms have no real existence independent of Brahman.

Proceeding logically from this starting point, it is possible to find satisfying solutions to the metaphysical and psychological questions that present themselves. Then, through the life of vichara, we may pass on from an intuitive understanding to the discovery in direct experience of the self-shining light and timeless Truth of our own Being, where no suffering or imperfection could ever appear.

Non-dual Meditation:
Am I Doing it Right?

It is often asked, how is meditation done? What is the right way to meditate? Every mind is different and we are constantly learning, so there cannot be one complete and final answer to this question. Still, however experienced or new we are to meditation, it is good to keep asking about how to do it best, otherwise we might find ourselves reinforcing unhelpful habits, or not meditating at all.

There are many forms of meditation. Here we are considering specifically meditation based on the non-dual teachings, which help us to understand that if we look deeply enough into ourselves, we find an underlying reality that is shared by everyone and everything. To know this in direct experience brings fulfilment and fearlessness.

All forms of meditation involve working with and on our mind, which is volatile and complicated, and so in meditation there must be techniques to manage the mind's dynamics and complexity. Yet the aim of meditation is to transcend technique; in fact it is to transcend completely the mind and all complexity. Technique is a way of doing something. What we ultimately seek in meditation is not doing but being—the being of our true innermost nature, the universal reality in all.

In meditation, as in all arts, the way to transcend technique is to master it. So it is necessary to begin with the foundations which are clear and relevant to all who take up the practice.

Firstly, what is the purpose of meditation? Why do we meditate at all? Here is one point where a simple answer is possible, and we have already touched on it. The aim of meditation is to help us progress on the path to happiness and the certainty that nothing can fundamentally disturb our well-being.

How does meditation help us in this? We might answer that through meditation we develop life-skills, such as the capacity for deep relaxation, firm concentration, creative intuition and active goodwill.

Meditation can help us gain such qualities. But they do not of themselves yield complete well-being. If we have succeeded in developing these psychological assets to an appreciable extent, we will know that they bring advantages in our professional and personal lives. But we will also have found that these advantages are not enough to secure lasting fulfilment. Why not? What deprives us of complete happiness, even in the most favourable circumstances?

The answer is fear. This may not be obvious, because our mind and the demands of our life are many-sided and allow us little mental space for self-understanding. Only after much reflection and life-experience do we find that what denies us true happiness, even amidst prosperity, is fear, often the non-specific background form of fear we call anxiety.

Is there a solution to fear? We may suggest that it is courage. Courage is the valuable and admirable ability to continue in the face of fear, but it can only resist fear up to a point, and does not entirely dispel fear and its dark shadow.

What is the root of fear? It springs from our experience of being separate. We experience ourselves as distinct and different from everyone and everything else, and so we live in fear of loss, harm and, ultimately, of death.

If fear arises from separation, fearlessness is to be found where there is no separation. Can there be in life an experience in which there is no separation—a state of being and consciousness that is not separate from the whole, where no shadow of anxiety might arise?

Yes, this is possible, and it is the goal of the non-dual practices. Separation is experienced in our mind, and specifically in separative thoughts. When those thoughts are withdrawn, nothing remains to obscure the truth that one reality pervades all phenomena. That reality is not separate from our own being and consciousness, and it is indivisible, fearless, perfect. True Self-knowledge once realised can never be lost or forgotten, because the non-dual Reality is revealed as our natural state.

Having indicated the ultimate purpose of meditation and the other practices, let us consider what is certain about how to meditate—the techniques that lead to transcendence.

What is most important is that we continue with meditation and do not allow changing moods to deflect us from the practice. So one essential principle is to do meditation regularly. This means that it is best to decide when we are going to meditate each day and for how long. For example, we might choose to meditate every day, before breakfast, for 15 minutes, for a week. After that, we can think again and make changes. If we proceed with meditation in this way, whatever mood we are in, we will really benefit. This is a big step in making the mind our helper, and freeing ourselves from the mind's ups and downs and other limitations.

The next point is about where to meditate. If possible, meditate in the same place each day, as that will create helpful associations. Choose a clean, quiet space where you are unlikely to be disturbed.

Related to where we meditate is the posture we choose. This is significant, but not complicated: sit on a cushion on the floor, or a firm chair, whichever is most stable and comfortable for you. As far as possible, keep the back and neck straight and upright, without straining at all.

We have thought about the time, place and posture for meditation and understood the importance of a regular rhythm. The final question is exactly what we are going to meditate on, that is, which practices we are going to do. This also is best decided in advance and kept to for a chosen period.

The meditation practices that follow are a set which could be taken up regularly. It is recommended to do a structured group of practices like this because it is unrealistic to think that we can leap straight into deep meditation. We have to take it step by step.

So our first practice is an inner preparation, and we are advised to begin each session in this way. What is the aim of this preparation? In daily life, we use our mind to manage what needs to be done. In meditation, it is our mind that has to be managed. And so what we call our attitude of mind needs to be adjusted with a preparation, such as this.

For a few moments, reflect on this thought: Life is precious. I am grateful for this life. I am grateful.

Breathing Practice

Because there is such a close connection between our breathing and our state of mind, it is often helpful to include a breathing practice in our meditation session, and we will do so here. This practice combines conscious breathing with a simple affirmation.

> Breathe a little more slowly and deeply than usual. When a rhythm of conscious breathing is established, then, with each in-breath say silently to yourself the word 'Here', and with each out-breath, 'Now'.

A practice like this helps to lift the mind out of its usual habits and become still and receptive. When it does, our experience is transformed. But there is no need to think about this. Whatever thoughts or questions come up, we practise simply stilling and centering the mind by keeping our attention on the breath and the words 'here', 'now'. Do this practice for four minutes.

Visualisation

The next of our techniques that lead to transcendence applies to our imagination.

> Visualise inwardly a line of light in the centre of your body, extending from the region of the navel to the top of the forehead. Use all your powers of imagination to visualise this line of light, then keep your attention focused on it.

The line of light draws our attention to the centre of our being and frees the mind from distracting thoughts. Our aim is to uncover within ourselves the stable, peaceful consciousness, which is always present, but generally overlooked. This practice gives help and protection in many ways. Do it for five minutes now.

Meditation on a Text

Having done our preparation, breathing practice and visualisation, we now come to meditation on a text pointing to the non-dual reality of our own ultimate nature.

> THE CONSCIOUS SELF IS THE
> SUPREME, INFINITE BLISS,
> AND THE SUPREME INFINITE
> BLISS IS NONE OTHER THAN
> MY CONSCIOUS SELF.

It was said at the beginning that the aim of meditation and life is happiness; that happiness is fearlessness, and fearlessness is found in the experience of non-separation. Here is the solution: when our true nature is revealed, we find that the innermost consciousness in us is identical with the infinite bliss we are seeking.

During the time of meditation, do not question the text, trust and affirm it. It concerns your own being at the deepest level.

Try not to be sleepy, or dreamy. Take a few deep breaths if needed to stay fully awake. Keep your attention on the text, and let its meaning gradually reveal itself as not separate from the light of your own being. Devote six minutes to this meditation.

Closing Practice

Like the preparation that we began with, a closing practice helps us to adjust, this time to taking up our active roles again. We want our daily meditation to be a special time, and also a natural part of our whole life. Ending our session with a closing practice helps to make it both. Focus for a few moments on this thought:

> May everyone, everywhere, find the place of non-separation within themselves.

Non-duality: Why Don't I Feel It?

There is a challenge that we are likely to encounter on the path concerning the gap there seems to be between our ideal, which promises fearlessness, fulfilment and perfect inner freedom, and our practical experience. We express this when we say things like: 'Non-duality makes sense, but I don't feel it. Theoretically, intellectually, I understand that all is one—that there are countless points of view but not more than one reality. How could it be otherwise? Yet, somehow, that is not how it seems for me. Shouldn't it make me free from anxiety, and enjoy a happy sense of oneness with the power behind everything? I don't. There is so much I cannot understand; I still get anxious and bad-tempered. I feel vulnerable, and sometimes just flat and empty. So am I missing something, or doing something wrong?'

Let us be reassured that it is natural and healthy to ask such questions. It shows that our interest is not merely academic. It is right to look for solutions in the one place where they can be found, that is, in the condition of our own mind. And it is good to be conscious of the powerful psychological energies at work within us, such as the will to feel good, because we want to harness and find the right channel for all these currents of thought and vitality. So is it possible to reconcile this apparent divide between what we might expect and hope non-duality will make us feel, and our actual experience?

First, we notice something essential about feelings and why they affect us so much, which is that feelings are constantly changing; it is in their nature to change. Like time and music and rivers and life, feelings are never still. Equally, what we call a 'good' feeling, or the 'right' feeling is ever-changing. Sometimes we want to feel complete peace. At other times we seek the good feeling of being creative and dynamic. At times we yearn for intense emotional involvement; at other times for the relief of easy light-heartedness. Sometimes we desire to feel significant, valued, influential; at other times to be totally unburdened. One day we want what is familiar, homely and personal; another day we are ready for adventure and new discoveries. Thus the essential nature of our human feelings is to change, and so too does what constitutes feeling 'good'.

In contrast, we have understood that the non-dual reality is beyond changes and limitations. As the ultimate totality of all that is, how could there be anything else, or any other form, that it could change into? And so we come to the conclusion that one cannot in fact 'feel' non-duality, because even at their best and highest, feelings include the certainty that they will pass. And whatever feels right and good just now, will also inevitably change.

In truth then, what we are seeking and longing for, and what the non-dual teaching assures us is there to be found, is something greater than thought and feeling, which will come to life as our enquiry progresses.

We might at first be disappointed or frustrated if we cannot find, or evoke within ourselves, an emotional response that matches the grandeur of the non-dual ideal. But this apparent failure does not mean that we are doing something wrong in our practice. It indicates a need to revise our expectations regarding what should follow from our practices. The will to feel good is constantly at work within us. We cannot and should not deny or ignore this essential human motivation. But the force of our emotions needs to be engaged in a way that will help to lead us through feelings to that which is greater than feeling—beyond limitations to the universal.

What is the way forward? Let us tackle it in two stages. The first is what we might call immediate self-help: techniques and tactics we can apply to our situation whatever it is right now. The second stage is our long-term strategy, how we can progress towards our ultimate goal.

Beginning with the first stage, a good way to help ourselves is often to take up again one of the practices we are doing at our regular meditation time. We can do a breathing practice or visualisation in almost any circumstances, and it may be possible to focus on the meditation text as well. By noticing our state of mind, stepping back from it, and focusing on one of these practices, we can effectively give our thoughts and feelings an upward turn.

Many visualisations and meditations involve light, and to think of light in any form is often a helpful strategy. When we notice dark thoughts in our mind or gloomy moods in our heart, if we find ourselves apparently at odds with others, to simply think of light within and around us will always bring benefits. The line of light practice described on page 97 is a traditional and particularly powerful application of this principle.

Light is symbolic and exemplary in many ways. We remember that light does not fight darkness, or argue with darkness. In fact, light has nothing to do with darkness at all.

Another quality of light is its apparent immediacy. Heat may take time to warm something up, effort needs time to produce a result, but the effect of light in our experience is immediate. Similarly, we do not need to wait for help to lift our mood. If we find ourselves waiting for something external to make us feel better, let us not forget that there is always something we can do for ourselves. In fact, only we can really help ourselves, and the good news is that we have the power to do so. We can always turn to light; it does not have to be a struggle or a fight. The one thing we do need to do, is to be alert to our inner state, which is another way of saying that we need to live consciously.

This brings us to what we called stage two, the search for a solution to the root cause of the problem, which is that although we have understood and accepted the idea of non-duality, we do not always 'feel' it, or rather do not experience what we would like or might expect non-duality to make us feel.

To solve this we must first ask ourselves: 'What do I really want? What is my first priority? What would make me entirely fulfilled?' We need to be careful not to ask, 'What do I think I should want most?' We have to frankly ask, 'What in fact do I want most? What do the images of happiness that arise in my imagination contain?'

If we discover that what comes first is an aspect of our material circumstances, that there is something in the world we feel we must attain or accomplish, then it is best to acknowledge that this is our true position now. Then we can consciously take practical steps in pursuit of that objective. Underlying all desires is hidden the ultimate desire for supreme Self-realisation. To energetically work towards our legitimate ambitions can benefit others and also exposes us to the life-experience from which we may learn valuable lessons.

The non-dual teachings will become relevant and meaningful to us when the answer to our question is: 'I enjoy the things that make life pleasant and rewarding, but I have also realised that none of these things are completely satisfying. What I am longing for is something that is free from change, everlasting and absolute. Only this can entirely fulfil me, and if necessary I will sacrifice other considerations for its sake.' When this is our sincere conviction, then we will begin to 'feel' the significance of non-duality.

What can we do to mature this realisation and have it colour and energise our whole psychology? Once again, we do not have to wait for something outside to bring relief. The feeling of separation belongs to our perception, not to the ultimate truth. We have understood this teaching theoretically; now it is for us to use all our powers of reason and imagination to affirm it. It does not help to hope that an external power or event will come and make everything look different. We have to make the changes for ourselves, by consciously directing our thoughts and feelings in order to realise what transcends all thoughts and feelings.

We began with a difficulty, expressed as frustration with how we may intellectually accept non-duality, but find that our state of mind does not reflect it. The answer has appeared as a restatement of the essential teachings: the root of all our difficulties is ignorance of our true nature, and the solution to this ignorance is knowledge through Self-realisation. The way to knowledge is enquiry, which begins with taming our mental impulses and then bringing our thoughts and emotions into harmony with the principle that our inmost self is pure consciousness and that consciousness underlies and reveals all phenomena. The divisions belong to a point of view, not Reality. This is the truth of the ever-blissful Self of all.

A Guiding Principle:
Does This Change?

In meditation and other practices we focus on symbols and statements which lead us towards the Reality that underlies appearances and where lasting fulfilment and security may be found.

In order to absorb ourselves in those symbols and statements, we have to develop a preliminary understanding of them, and we do this through enquiry, in Sanskrit *Vichara*, which means listening to, and then reflecting on, the non-dual teachings as presented by an illumined source.

Here the question arises of how can we understand the reality of which the mind is a fragment? When we see how far the implications of this question go, and realise the limited range of our usual methods of investigating things, then we become seekers of universal truth.

There is a guiding principle that will always help in our enquiry. This principle is simple, yet profound and challenging in its implications. It is that ultimate reality, the highest truth, does not change. Whatever we encounter in our vichara, let us ask: does this change? If so, we can be sure that it is not the complete and final truth. The great lesson to be learned from everything that changes is: keep on, keep going, this is not yet your highest goal. Equally, wherever we find indications or evidence of something that is free of change, we may be confident that this is worthy of further investigation in our quest for deeper knowledge and fulfilment.

Let us consider how we can apply this guiding principle. First, we may ask, do we find anything in our experience that does not change?

Our initial response might be, no, nothing does not change. If we look around with open eyes, or through telescopes and microscopes, our whole life-experience teaches that everything changes, change is what is real. And we may be inclined to add that this is all for the good, because change is what makes life interesting and progressive.

But has our investigation so far been adequate and complete? Let us note carefully that in our experience there are two elements: there is everything that we experience, all that comes through our senses and our mental reactions; and there is also the consciousness to which all this is revealed. That which is experienced is certainly ever-changing, yet the one who is aware of all this, is unchanging. Our consciousness witnesses all that changes equally, and is itself unchanged.

According to our temperament, the truth and importance of this conclusion may impress us in different ways. If we have a rational, analytic turn of mind, we might become logically convinced that in order to perceive all the changing objects, there must be a perceiver that does not change. Or we may be more emotionally centered and somehow just be intuitively certain that: 'There is something unchanging in me; otherwise I would not be me.' These intimations are right. We have found an essential element of experience that does not change, and it is our consciousness—our awareness.

To put that another way, we have found that what does not change is our true Self, our own innermost

Being. Our body changes, our mind changes, but the one who witnesses all this change, the I am, is beyond change. This is why our enquiry can lead towards complete Self-realisation and well-being that nothing can take away, even as we come towards the end of our life.

Having looked within, let us ask again, is there anything in the world around us that is permanent, untouched by the flux of change? All aspects of nature, from subatomic events to galaxies, display changing states. But what do we find if we turn our attention from the parts to the whole, to the totality in which all the parts exist? Total reality, the complete whole, is what has been referred to as the Absolute, supreme Being, God, in Sanskrit, *Brahman*. We cannot think of this in the way we think of separate things. Yet this Brahman is of supreme interest because in it we live and move and have our being.

How might we approach direct knowledge of the Absolute? Where are we to look? Here we see the need for special care and guidance in our enquiry. Usually, the word 'where' means where in space and time. But on reflection we understand that Reality does not come into being at a moment in time and a place in space, because that would suggest that time-space existed before Reality.

The supreme Truth therefore is not limited by space and time. We say that it is infinite, meaning not that it is infinitely large or long-lasting, but that it transcends space and time entirely. And where time does not apply, change cannot arise. Absolute Reality is transcendent and immutable.

How, we may ask, does this world of variety and change come to be, if the total reality which is apparently its ultimate source and substratum, is never touched by time and change? This question has occupied and defied philosophers for millennia, and the answer cannot be encapsulated in thought or words. The way to deeper knowledge is to look within, not to ideas and objects that are separate from us, but towards that constant awareness to which, and in which, the ideas and objects appear. What we can explore directly, in inner quietude, is our own consciousness, and the contents of experience, and how they appear to be related.

The consummation of this enquiry, rightly guided, is the highest Self-knowledge. That will reveal to us the truth about the apparent connection between our Self and what we experience; and it will also reveal the truth of the apparent relation between the absolute, supreme Being, and the finite, phenomenal world.

The ultimate fact underlying all our meditations and practices is that our true Self is not essentially different from the supreme Being. The apparent differences and separations arise when all is viewed from a particular point in space and time. In reality, there are no points of view, no gaps or separations.

At first we hear these indications from an illumined source. If we wish to pursue these ideas, we use our powers of reflection, and our feeling for beauty and harmony, to absorb and understand them in principle. Then at the meditation time, we take the subjects for our meditation as an explorer takes a compass, and we turn our whole attention in one-pointed focus on what the symbols and statements indicate.

At every step we will be saved from many delays and dead ends if we remember the guiding principle, that the highest reality does not change. For example, we may find an idea forming in our mind of the supreme Being, the ultimate source and sustainer of the world. Then, let us ask: 'Does this, as I have conceived it, ever change, could that ever change?' Similarly, as we investigate the inner light of our own awareness, we might ask: 'What I have discovered so far—does this change; could this change?'

At times we may be visited by apparently unusual experiences, and wonder: 'What does this mean? Is it important? How can I get it back? Does it make me special?' It is easy to become preoccupied by such matters, which are all ultimately productions of the unquiet mind. At all such times, we may simply ask ourselves: 'Is this changing? Could it ever change?' If so, pass on. It may teach a lesson, but is not the final destination.

All of life is enhanced if we learn to lightly and lovingly allow everything that changes to go and pass on. And if we pursue the inner enquiry, treating everything with due respect and love, while binding ourselves to nothing finite, we will find a new light and transparency dawning within, revealing the

Reality beyond thoughts and words, fulfilling our deepest needs and infinitely surpassing them, our own ultimate being.

How Can My Self Be the All?

The teaching at the heart of non-duality is that if we enquire deeply enough we will discover that our true nature, our real self, is not in essence different from the supreme Being, the ultimate reality of all. This identity is the basis of the non-dual meditations and it is what makes possible the direct experience of reality called enlightenment, which is the fulfilment of our deepest longings.

This should prompt us to reflect deeply, because when we first consider such ideas, we notice, not identity, but seemingly unbridgeable differences between the individual and the whole. Our human condition, our most pressing hopes and anxieties, spring from the apparent certainty that we have been born at a particular time and place, and will one day pass away. So the suggestion that the individual and the universal are ultimately not different in nature, is a direct challenge to our conventional ways of seeing. How are we to understand this rightly? Can there be identity between the individual and the universal?

First, let us examine our conception of the great truth, the universal reality, the ultimate goal of all our seeking. This is what has been called the Absolute, the Transcendental, the supreme Being, God; in the non-dual philosophy it is referred to by the Sanskrit name, Brahman. We immediately encounter a challenge here because what these words indicate is entirely beyond the finite forms that the mind can think of or imagine.

When we try to think of the Absolute, we inevitably approach it through what we can relate to, which is our own life and the world we see around us. And so we conceive of the supreme reality as the ultimate source, arbiter and sustainer of all phenomena. Whether our outlook is coloured by religion, philosophy or science, our conception of ultimate reality involves its pre-eminence in relation to the known universe.

This may arouse a sense of reverence, even awe, for the supreme power behind the world-appearance, which is entirely appropriate and is one reason why the teaching on identity has to be rightly understood.

And yet, we need to remember that any idea of the supreme Being that is based on its apparent relation to the world we experience, is far from the absolute reality, which has no relation to anything finite. Being the infinite All, how could there be anything else that it would relate to.

It is true that the world as we know it is full of separations and boundaries and gaps. But these divisions belong to our mental apparatus, not to Reality itself. So when we think of the supreme Being as the creator and sustainer of the world, we project onto it limitations which in fact arise from our imperfect vision.

Is there anything that can be rightly conceived about the Absolute, God, Brahman? It may be said, with due care, that Brahman is being-consciousness-bliss. When everything that is contingent and limited is put aside, what remains is pure being, pure consciousness and pure bliss.

To be clear, these are not qualities or adjectives that apply to Brahman and could be separated from it, like the sun and its radiance, which will eventually fade. Brahman is absolute Being, and absolute Being is Brahman. Absolute consciousness and absolute Bliss have the same meaning.

What is the value and significance of this teaching for us now? Is it just abstract philosophy? Is it the exalted, but far distant goal of transcendental enquiry? In truth, nothing could be closer or more immediately relevant to us than existence-consciousness-bliss, rightly understood.

We found that our conception of the supreme Being included elements that have been imposed by our habitual modes of thought. Now let us ask if there is anything out of place in our understanding of our self, of our own nature?

The initial and conventional view is that our self means the one who acts, and who experiences the outcome of those actions and the flow of events in the world. My self, on this view, is the individual, who depends on some things, is indifferent to others, who hopes, fears, tries, suffers and rejoices. But does this way of thinking about our self get to the heart of the matter? Does it distinguish what is truly our self from everything else?

When, for example, we hope or fear, we conceive of something or someone, together with feelings of attraction or aversion regarding that object. And when we are active, we are aware of events in the world, in which our words and movements participate. So our wants, anxieties and efforts incorporate objects external to us, which exist and change in ways that have no relation to our self.

To truly apprehend our self, we have to distinguish self from our most intimate cares and deliberate actions. If we persist with this inner enquiry, what remains when all that is not-self has been left aside? There is revealed as our own being, that which can never be negated, which is self-revealed, which cannot be divided. To put that positively, there is pure being, pure consciousness and the total absence of suffering—bliss.

Brahman, the ultimate Reality, and our true Self, which is called in Sanskrit Atman, are the final goal of all our seeking. When we enquire into both, under the light of right guidance, and exclude everything that is not essential and belongs to the world of appearances, we find that Brahman and Atman are identical as being-consciousness-bliss.

The previous chapter considered the guiding principle that the highest truth does not change. Anything that changes teaches us to pass on to our real goal. Now we can further refine this vital insight. When we leave aside all that changes, our meditations and enquiries will pass on from forms that exist, to existence; from conscious beings, to consciousness; from finitude to bliss. This is the way to Atman-realisation.

We might ask, if the focus of our enquiry is exclusively Atma-Brahman—being-consciousness-bliss—then, where does this leave the world, the plane of nature and our lives? Is all this to be dismissed as irrelevant or insignificant?

No, to say so would be a misunderstanding. In fact, the non-dual perspective leaves the phenomenal world exactly where it seems to be.

What we call common sense tells us that the world presses upon us, that appearances are often misleading, and that we have to cope with life as best we can. Scientific investigation reveals that some aspects of nature are predictable and controllable; some are not, and that appearances are different from what underlies them.

The non-dual perspective does not contradict common sense or the results of scientific investigation. In fact, non-dual practice helps us to develop the inner resources needed to follow both common sense and empirical investigations consistently.

Non-duality distinguishes between the reality-status of the world as it appears in our experience, and the ultimate, infinite Truth. And it presents the possibility of complete fulfilment through true knowledge of Self as being-consciousness-bliss.

The knowledge of the identity of Atman and Brahman, and the truth about the apparent relationship of the non-dual reality to appearances, is unlike any other kind of knowledge. Here there is no distinction between the knower and the known. That is why the liberating, direct knowledge of Reality is possible and, in a vital sense, is always true.

Another question may arise. Because this enquiry into our own nature distinguishes so acutely between Self and not-Self, could it make us cold, isolated and uncaring towards people and the world around us?

It is true that this path of self-discovery does strengthen our psychological independence. And it helps us to discern what really is our own responsibility from what misplaced social conventions may seem to impose upon us. But all this makes us more, not less, genuinely caring and empathetic. The precious quality we call human sensitivity arises precisely because all minds are lit by the one eternal consciousness. You are that infinite consciousness.

As we progress on the path, and increasingly discern what is essential to our being from what is derivative and changeable, our compassion and sense of oneness will heighten correspondingly. And when the bliss of true self-realisation dawns, the light within is revealed as the light which lights the way and the goal for all humanity.

Is Non-duality Incompatible
with Human Love?

We may have heard that on the path to enlightenment it is necessary to free ourselves from desires and preferences that bind us to particular people or things and distract us from what is universal and eternal. And we might have understood that to progress towards inner illumination we need to revise our understanding of what we are; that we should let go of the feeling that I am my mind and my emotions, and instead be convinced that the real Self is the one being and light in all.

If we have heard such indications, we may wonder whether applying the non-dual teachings means that we have to give up love, if love involves strong feelings and special connections with other human beings.

This might make us ask ourselves whether we wish to pursue the non-dual enquiry. And we may even wonder if there could be something misguided about teachings that seem to be incompatible with human love.

When such questions arise in our mind, it is best to think them through clearly. So we need to ask, firstly, 'What is love?'; secondly, 'What is non-duality?', and then we can consider how they are related.

What then do we mean by love? Often, when we say we love something or someone it means that we intensely like or enjoy them. Sometimes, love means a kind of identification; it is the feeling that the loved one is almost inseparable from us, part of what we are.

If we take much pleasure in something, we are willing to sacrifice other concerns for its sake, perhaps without even thinking that it is a sacrifice at all. This is an important lesson on the path to wisdom.

The feeling of being inseparable from the beloved, is exemplified in a mother's tenderness for a new-born child, and is occasionally experienced in romantic encounters. These forms of human love appear as symbols of beauty and transformative power in art and literature. They present the possibility of finding absorption in a whole that transcends the boundaries of narrow individuality.

Next then, what is the non-dual view of life and the world? It is that all our questions and difficulties arise because of an incomplete and faulty understanding of our own true nature. What is the ultimate Truth about our nature? It is that our real Self—our I—is the Self of all that ever was, is, and ever will be. This Self cannot be contained in any thought or theory, but it can be known directly as the uncaused cause or the unsustained sustainer of the mind and all experience.

The practical path involves understanding these teachings in principle and adjusting our priorities, thoughts and actions accordingly. Then through inner enquiry and meditation new light is allowed into our inner world. The final goal, the ultimate discovery, is enlightenment, and it may also be called infinite bliss.

We have already seen ways in which human beings can learn dedication and self-expansion through the experience of love, understood as both an intense liking and a deep bond. But there may be some anxiety in our mind that at a certain stage on the inner path we will be required to renounce fervent enjoyments and enduring bonds in order to pass on towards the summit, the direct experience of the one reality in all.

One thing is certain. We can be sure that we will never have to give up an attitude of loving kindness to humanity in general. According to all the well-known moral codes, the ideal is benevolent goodwill to everyone equally, whether they are friends or opponents, family or strangers. Similarly, we need not fear that one day we might be called on to abandon love of ideals like justice or peace; nor is there any reason to think that we might have to forgo dedication to a good cause, such as charity, science, learning, art, public service or creative enterprise.

But the noble injunction that we should love all equally, may heighten the concern that we might be prohibited from loving someone in particular. And while it is certainly possible to love an ideal or cause, love for human beings is a special case because then their life and emotions are involved: we may be loved in return.

In order to fully resolve the concerns that have been raised, we must ask whether, in following the non-dual teachings towards their final conclusion, there will come a point where it is necessary to cease having special, loving relations with individual human beings.

The answer in brief, is no. Mutually supportive human relationships are not incompatible with any phase of the non-dual teachings. A belief that they are incompatible might arise from two misunderstandings. One is the idea that some essential and natural features of human life are intrinsically impure and obstructive to the development of our highest potentials. This is not so. All forms of healthy vitality can be expressed wisely and progressively.

The other misunderstanding is that love and what is called detachment or inner independence, are opposites. In fact, pure love and right detachment are facets of one priceless treasure.

As we saw, the great challenge to which the non-dual teachings offer a response is that so long as we lack inner illumination, we have an incomplete and distorted view of reality and in particular of our own nature. This is because all our experience comes through our individual mind, which is a detail in reality and capable of grasping only fractions of the whole.

So whereas reality is one and undivided, we experience myriad limitations and divisions. At the centre of this experience is the view of our self as a separate conscious entity, isolated from the whole, and defined by the limitations of the mind. The essential truth is that the gaps and limitations belong to appearances, not reality. Our own true nature is the infinite reality, not the apparent separation.

Is it possible to transcend the range of the mind and discover our identity with the infinite? Yes, it is, because of the vital truth that ultimate reality is consciousness absolute—the only conscious factor in all experience. Our own consciousness, our Self, is not in essence different from that universal consciousness, the substratum of the mind and all experience, and can be revealed as such through the practice of discernment and inner enquiry, rightly guided.

Now let us consider this suggestion: 'In order to know our true self, it is necessary to give up relationships with other people, and to live in solitude or a special community.'

To say this would imply that there is something fundamentally different about each of those circumstances, but this cannot be the non-dual teaching. To assert, for example, that sharing a home with a life-partner could prevent us from knowing ultimate reality, or that living in a hermitage might help us to do so, is to say that the shared home and the hermitage each have a connection with reality, a connection that is helpful in one case and obstructive in the other.

In truth, as we saw, the supreme reality has no real connection with anything finite: being infinite and undivided, how could there be something else for it to be connected to? The finite forms we experience through our mind differ essentially from the infinite reality beyond the mind, and this applies to all phenomena equally: it cannot be said that some situations are closer to, or further from, ultimate reality than others. It is not the circumstances that determine the inner path we follow. Whether we choose, or find ourselves in, partnerships or solitude or community, we may continue to believe that we are defined by the roles our body and mind play in the world, or we can pursue the enquiry into our deeper nature.

The practical path then involves looking on the mind as something other than our innermost Self. This is what is meant by being detached from our thoughts and feelings and not identified with them. What does this imply for our relations with those around us? Could it make us indifferent and cold?

No, because being detached and disidentified from our mind and body does not mean not caring about them. In fact this objectivity helps us to understand the true value of our body and mind: the ultimate liberation is possible in a human life, and nowhere else. This heightened appreciation of what is most valuable in our physical and mental nature will extend to those around us and enhance those relationships, not impair them.

It is human nature to care about what affects us personally. Some people affect us deeply and intimately, and where they do so positively, we find what is called love. It follows that those who do not touch our lives in this way, remain outside the circumference of our affection. And if it happens that we cease to feel positively affected, that our wants and needs are no longer being fulfilled, then commitment and love are seen to fade. This is why human relationships have all the scope they do for gladness and also sadness.

Through our enquiry and meditation practices we grow in understanding and the firm conviction that what is most truly our Self is the inner conscious essence, and this becomes the centre of our attention and care. Then naturally we will be closest on this innermost level to those with whom we share our personal lives. The fabric of our relationships will be interwoven with what cannot change, where there can be no decline or lack of fulfilment.

There is then nothing fundamentally wrong with caring most for what affects us personally. From it we learn the paramount truth that Self is the object of the highest love. This great lesson sets us on the way to fulfilling life's highest potential, direct knowledge of our true Self as the infinite supreme Being.

As we approach this, loving those around us as our self ceases to be a distant ideal, and becomes the living truth. Then we know that love is not something that we do or have. Love is what we are.

How Can Non-duality Help Me Now?

Non-duality can help us now by showing where to find four precious and life-giving resources. These are: a refuge, a foundation, a direction and a purpose.

Where do these boons come from? Their source is Reality itself, non-dual, one without a second. This source is transcendental, but in the world of relativity we encounter it in the form of teachings, recorded in ancient texts, and presented in the language of our time, by those who have discovered the essence in themselves and thus apparently assumed the role of teachers, although no sense of agency can truly be attributed to them. Behind the texts and the teachers, non-duality is a universal, impersonal, living truth and supreme power, phenomenally emanating from the source of creation, and from the centre of our own being.

The teachings thus reach us through words which convey information and good news about ourselves. They disclose that we are living under the burden of a misapprehension regarding our own situation. Until now, our human consciousness has revealed to us a world of opportunities and dangers, together with some limited and fragile capacities that we have been granted in order to survive and perhaps prosper. We attain or achieve moments of well-being and happiness, but these prove incomplete and impermanent. We feel a want of security, strength, purpose and fulfilment, and so a cloud of anxiety hangs over us. There seems to be no solution to this difficulty beyond endurance or distraction, which we can sustain only by drawing on inner resources that dwindle just as our need becomes more pressing with the passing years.

The non-dual teachings can guide us to that source of security, strength, purpose and fulfilment. On the way, an obstacle must be overcome. This obstacle is more apparent than real, but it gains stature from an effective disguise. The obstacle is a preconception, which prevents us from hearing the teachings, or rather, worse, it distorts and dilutes their meaning. This expectation assumes the disguise of 'being realistic', but in fact stems from ignorance of Reality.

The assumption is that non-duality will be another assemblage of ideas and strategies, similar to those we have already encountered—some related to our religious heritage, others presenting themselves as innovations—all purporting to make the most of those fragile and limited capacities to survive, prosper and endure our situation. This presumption is dignified as an attitude of realism, because so far we have not been able to form an idea of anything greater.

The non-dual philosophy is presented in combination with practical teachings. Our pre-conceptions cause us to misunderstand the goal of these techniques and to believe that they are further ways to make the best of our circumstances. In fact, the intended outcome of these methods, rightly applied, is that we will be enabled to receive and absorb the full meaning of the non-dual teaching. This essential message is not how to cope with our situation, but that our true position is entirely other than we currently believe it to be. This is because from the highest standpoint the world of opportunities and dangers is a phenomenal appearance, not the absolute truth. Our real nature is not a part of the phenomenal world and its constrictions, but the consciousness in which the universe of forms appears. This consciousness is our ultimate Self, and is not distinct from the infinite, eternal, unbound, supreme Being.

In order to assimilate this revelation we require inner qualities including the capacity for voluntary mental quiescence and sustained one-pointed concentration. These resemble skills prescribed by those schools of personal development whose purpose is to enhance our individual condition, rather than to transcend it completely. Thus our preconceptions lead us to mistake the means for the end, and the teachings bring no relief of our fundamental problem. It is only when we have been brought to a point of readiness by much experience of life, that a fresh possibility emerges, from an unexpected and hitherto disprised source: the very disappointment we have been trying to hide from ourselves. When all attempts to find happiness by enhancing our individual inner resources have failed, and the approach of despair removes the wish, or ability, to deny that failure, then we may be receptive to a message which is not a variation on anything our mind has, or could have, formulated before, and the true import of the teachings makes some impression on our understanding.

Now there appears before us a further divide between our present standpoint and the objective, as we understand it. We may intuitively recognise, or intellectually accept, that the non-dual teaching on the essential identity of the human and the transcendent, does follow from the principle and that the whole transcends the parts, and that reality differs from appearances. But this rational consent is accompanied by a sense of regret. Direct knowledge that the individual consciousness is not in essence different from the Universal, may be, we acknowledge, in principle possible for rare spiritual heroes. But, we confess, it is certainly beyond the scope of our own, quite ordinary, capabilities.

Yet once again, the apparent defeat arises from a misapprehension regarding what is required and expected of us. We imagine that we must somehow journey across the vastness that seems to separate us from the mountain peak, a journey for which our reserves of strength and navigation skills are sadly inadequate. But this assessment is the offspring of what has been exposed as a primal error, and it is distracting us from the real task ahead. That task is to unlearn the lessons which have convinced us that we are no more than a mind and body striving to survive. The mind-body is a particle in the cosmos which appears in Being-Consciousness. Our true Self is that which reveals and transcends the coming and going of every particle.

The need is not to bring about a marvel, but to remove the veils that obscure the living Truth. This is the ultimate challenge of life, but the means necessary to meet it are available, and not only to an exceptional few. What may prevent us from recognising and employing those means, is a continued belief that life, that is, the life of a body and mind in the world, can yield enduring satisfaction, and that if it has not done so yet, this is because we have not explored and exhausted all its possibilities. As long as we project this expectation onto all experience, the universe will provide us with opportunities for further exploration, and the highest teaching and wisdom, for us, must be regarding how to make the fullest use of those opportunities.

The determination to seek and discover fulfilment in the world revealed by our mind and senses, may be sustained by our currently incomplete understanding of the wisdom teachings. There we find reasons, and perhaps courage, to persevere with the search, and also further grounds to fear that if we have not succeeded, it is merely because our individual efforts so far have been insufficient, and therefore we must, once again, try harder.

At this point, our need for a refuge, foundation, direction and purpose, is becoming urgent. Our efforts appear to lead only in circles. We are obliged now to consider the possibility that there is something fundamental about which we are mistaken, and that this mistake enters into all our efforts to do and to understand what is best. The willingness to consider this possibility of an error in the fabric of our world-view, is the embryo of teachability, which is another name for humility. Now it is possible that we will listen to, and hear, the non-dual teaching, without holding up an internal wall against the subtle and liberating message at its centre.

That message is adapted to our capacity and presented with two aspects. One is an indication of the supreme Truth, which is our Self; it cannot be otherwise, because ultimately there is nothing else. The second is what, by implication, our true nature is not. The first is necessarily no more than a pointer, and initially its main purpose is to help us understand the second, regarding what Self is not, and this can be stated more definitely: Self is not anything finite.

The mind, being attracted always to whatever it interprets as favourable to itself, attends first to the positive indication of transcendental identity, which produces a spark of interest, but the usual mental faculties cannot be engaged in it, and the appeal tends to give way to aridity. If our need is urgent enough, interest is sustained by what remains, the apparently negative aspect of the teaching, and again vital potentialities come to light where least expected. Still functioning according to its survival instincts, the mind at last finds reasons to believe that its failures and disappointments have not been entirely due to inadequate efforts or personal misfortune, but because the world accessible to our senses and mind does not contain what it was looking for. We recognise, or at least consider, the truth that if complete security and fulfilment are to be found, it cannot be in the realm of forms and change. This gives meaning and relevance to the indication at the apex of the teachings: that the non-dual absolute, the supreme Brahman, where there is no divide between subject and object or between substance and appearance, alone is entirely Real. And that is the Self to be known.

This meaningful conception of what would ultimately fulfil us, and what cannot, is called 'discernment of the Real', and it is an essential item of equipment for every seeker of Self-knowledge. It is not the goal, but it can be used at any time to provide a refuge, which will shelter, and not detain, a traveller on the way.

With discernment comes revaluation. We have long known that what is attractive does not always lead to happiness, and we have understood the wisdom teaching to be that we should practise detachment, or at least restraint, regarding what is unconducive to our overall welfare. But what is the highest good, and how to attain it, remains uncertain. Our strength and balance are strained by conflicting desires and demands, and the difficulties are compounded by self-reproach over perceived failures to decide and do what is right. Our own defences and preconceptions deflect our efforts, until we discern that the world revealed to the senses does not contain the whole Truth or the completeness we have been seeking. With this discernment comes true detachment, which is not from features of the world, but detachment from the belief that anything that changes could ever free us from fear and want.

The mind, moved by a genuine desire to help but a flawed understanding of how to do so, will repeatedly re-assert its conviction that lasting happiness can be composed from the materials within its scope. With determined ingenuity, it will initiate and justify fresh attempts, and revel in the distractions that follow. Therefore, to sustain detachment does require effort, but when our diligence and restraint are guided by discernment, it is possible. In turn, discernment is refined in the quietened mental environment provided by detachment, which is therefore said to be another prerequisite for the seeker of Self-realisation. Now we have a refuge, and also a foundation on which to build it. The attractions of the sense-world, instead of depleting our energy or distracting us, will be a source of inner nourishment and joy, as we see through their transient beauty, towards the wholeness that transcends them.

Discernment and detachment bring us to reconsider the lessons we learn during our attempts to find satisfaction in the world and in pursuit of the attractive. Chief among those lessons are: the value of being selective in what we think about and where we engage our senses; that moderation in our expectations reduces the likelihood of disappointment; and that well-informed advice is likely to prove a better guide than our raw impulses and inclinations. We look on these measures as compromises, but accept them as our best chance of avoiding unnecessary suffering. And we understand the wisdom teachings to be codifying the results of this experience, and extolling selectivity, moderation, and obedience to good counsel, as exemplary disciplines.

Applying these conclusions brings some advantages, including a feeling of personal respectability. But the benefits are limited. Our fundamental problems remain unsolved and we find ourselves still afflicted by insecurities and anxiety. This failure weakens our confidence in the teachings, and our incentive to sustain the discipline, while our need for reassurance and guidance heightens as the span of life remaining to us diminishes.

But the real failing is in regarding the teachings as mere restatements of the conclusions drawn from life-experience: that restraint and discipline should be exercised in practical matters in order to avoid mistakes and mishaps, and to extract traces of happiness from its sources in the world, as a skilled miner patiently separates the gold from the mass of dull ore. The non-dual teachings are more interior than this, and those disciplines are to be applied chiefly in the treatment of our mind. The practices of directing our thoughts and the rest are not a conduit for worldly consolations; their foremost purpose is to enable us to keep in focus whichever aspects of the non-dual philosophy are relevant to us at each moment.

Only the Absolute is absolutely real; appearances are incomplete and misleading. This truth never changes, whether we are engaged in meditation or mundane tasks, and however sunny or stormy the prevailing conditions may be. But to remain aware of this fact, and to express its implications by our thoughts and actions, requires constant inner adjustments, which we make by directing our mind and senses, practising moderation and endurance, and following wise counsel once we have assimilated it. This is not to accept a compromise; it is to affirm the highest of all potentialities. Thus the ability to guide the mind is true inner wealth, and it fulfils a further requirement for the seeker of Self-realisation. As well as a refuge and a foundation, we now have a working sense of direction.

Are we now in possession of all that was needed and all that the teachings had to offer? We are ready for a life of journeying and enquiry, but with this comes the possibility that we shall once again mistake the means for the ends and allow our assets to become impediments. We may find some felicity and comfort in the role of a traveller and lose sight of the need to reach the destination. To have a destination is to acknowledge that something is lacking in our present position, and we would prefer not to have the quality of our life spoiled by such dissatisfaction. We also know that to strive towards a destination requires effort, and that effort involves some discomfort, in overcoming natural inertia as well as the acceptance that something is missing. To fully recognise that there is a goal, is also to expose oneself to the fear of failure. Thus awareness of the need to reach an objective brings once more a sense of strain on our inner resources and balance, and now there is a possibility of evading despair by turning our attention from the objectives of an enquirer to the distractions of a tourist.

Here the creative mind is likely to find a particularly appealing opportunity to help, and the dangers of a wrong turn at this point might be avoided only if we are fortunate enough, and receptive enough, to receive trustworthy guidance. Noticing that to have a destination is to be in want, the mind can point to that phase of the non-dual teaching which asserts the ever-established identity of our true self and the

Absolute, and concludes that it would be a mistake to affirm that there remains a distance between oneself and the ideal. To say that the goal has not been attained, is to revert to the forms of faith which insist that the highest is a mystery unknowable in the present and that it is impious to seek it here: so reasons the mind that has appointed itself guardian of logical rigour. The intellect thus finds a way to dismiss as they arise any calls to strive for substantial change or progress, and this, the mind assures itself, is the proper use of the skills and refinements it has so far acquired.

However plausibly it may be presented, the inadequacy of this position must become apparent eventually, as our underlying anxieties persist and our energies ebb away. With deepening discernment it is understood that the non-dual teachings do affirm that Reality is always real and that our own nature is at one with it, but the teachings also recognise how this is hidden from us.

What hides the truth is, necessarily, other than truth, and may therefore be characterised as 'illusory' or 'unreal', but this does not negate the fact that we experience separation and suffer the bonds of limitation. From this comes an intense desire to be free of not-knowing. This formulation is precise and complete: it is an intense desire for liberation from wrong and incomplete knowledge of our own nature. Because it is a desire to be free of an error, this desire does not contradict the eternal non-dual truth which the intellect recognises in theory, while it does provide the motive force needed to overcome inertia. Knowing that we are dealing with an appearance, not ultimate reality, obviates the fear of acknowledging the challenge, and reassures us that here no effort is ever wasted. With this acquiescence we become aware that a subtle attraction is now acting on our inner being. We cease to hope that a mighty power will help us in our distress, and resolve instead to know Beauty Absolute revealed as our true Self.

It was said that the non-dual teachings constitute the visible aspect of a living force emanating from the source of all life, and that this force acts upon whatever is sensitive to it, whether we realise it or not. Exposed to the light, our disappointments, resignation, compromises and nascent despair have grown into discernment, right detachment, a sense of direction, and a supreme purpose that does not deny the eternal truth. We are now endowed with the potential to flourish at every stage of the path to Self-realisation. This is how non-duality will help us now.